Here's what dads 

Dad's Class

"American families are in crisis. At a time when 25 million American children (one in three kids) are growing up without their dads, Dennis Nun provides practical suggestions in *Dad's Class* for those men committed to being involved in the lives of their children. It is a must read for men who desire to be responsible and committed dads."

Gregg Nicklas CEO
Christian Heritage Children's Home

"I have known Dennis Nun for over 25 years. What makes this book so powerful is that it is not just empty words. He has lived, applied, and experienced what he has written in his own family. His words are insightful, practical, real and honest. I have already passed on some of these lessons from his journey to others. This book will be a critical tool in the hands of many fathers, like myself, who need all the help we can get."

Tim Bohlke
Founder of Harbor Ministries and
Director of the RYTHMinTWENTY Program

"Dennis Nun condenses decades of parenting experience into a fast and easy read. As a new father, these creative ways to impart life lessons are priceless nuggets of wisdom."

Mawi Asgedom
Speaker, Educator, Author and Founder of Mental Karate

"I have found that *Dad's Class* is one of the most important tools to come along, for helping strengthen family relationships and offering a legacy-building process for generations to come. *Dad's Class* is full of common sense that is often overlooked in our society. Dennis Nun has captured the essence of what it means to lead your children, by instilling in them values laden with sound wisdom and a process for making good decisions. I would recommend *Dad's Class* to every new and existing father. Whether your children are newborn or in their twenties, there is much to be gained by initiating your own Dad's Class with your sons and daughters."

Barry Lockard
President, Corhnhusker Bank & father of two

"*Dad's Class* is a resource that every dad should own. The practical principles and suggestions will help you be more effective in your role as a father. As a dad myself, I have the responsibility to prepare my four sons for life. This book challenges me to think more intentionally about my parenting. I am excited to begin implementing the concepts to parent more effectively. You and your kids will benefit from the valuable insights contained in this book."

Bryan Carlson
Executive Director, Southeast Nebraska Youth For Christ

"*Dad's Class* should be required reading for every—and I mean every—father in America. Our role as a dad goes well beyond just being the bread winner and protector. Our sons and daughters need fathers that are fully engaged in their lives if they are to become healthy, happy and productive adults. *Dad's Class* provides the framework for those meaningful discussions and life lessons. A must read!"

Dave Boon
Mentor, Motivator, Speaker and
Author of My Wish: Don't Get Swept Away as a Teen

"*Dad's Class* is relevant to the current crisis involving the lack of parenting in our country. I would recommend it to any parent or coach as an excellent resource."

Dr. Tom Osborne
Former Coach of the Nebraska Cornhuskers, UNL Athletic Director and Founder of The Teammates™ Mentoring Program.

"Of all the goals I have accomplished, being a father and seeing my children succeed has been the most rewarding. Parenting is a continual adventure and Dennis Nun's excellent book *Dad's Class* provides an invaluable map to follow that enables you to make the trip enjoyable with determination and purpose."

Dr. John Goddard
World Explorer - Author of The Survivor and Kayaks Down the Nile

"*Dad's Class* is a concise and poignant book which reminds us of a simple truth: Dads Matter! Dennis Nun has distilled his experience and passion in an easy to read format which will help fathers strengthen their relationships with their children. *Dad's Class* challenges us to review our priorities and consider how we can improve in the role of Dad. I heartily recommend this book! I know you will benefit greatly from reading *Dad's Class* and using it as a tool to strengthen your family."

Ken Canfield, Ph. D.
Founder, National Center for Fathering
Director of Boone Center for the Family at Pepperdine

Here's what young adults are saying about

Dad's Class

"Growing up going through Dad's Class I learned a lot of things I was never taught in school. I feel it better prepared me for the business world and has given me knowledge that my peers are still learning."

Adam Nun, Age 26

"Dad's Class has helped me in many ways, although I probably don't see all of them now. To have that time to talk about anything with my father is something so rare! Learning about business and good money management and how to be conservative in these areas is not something we were taught in school. I learned things that aren't routinely taught anywhere else. I feel like I understand how to make better choices, and how those choices can positively affect my life and allow me to be the kind of father who can justify his actions to his children. Those are character qualities I seek to carry over with my family. I feel like I better understand what it means to be a man."

Jordan Nun, Age 23

"Now that I am in college, I have come to appreciate the money management skills Dad's Class taught me. Living on my own has forced me to take responsibility of my finances, and the knowledge I gained in Dad's Class has helped tremendously in that area. In addition, what I learned about goal setting has motivated me as I pursue my education and look toward future jobs. Perhaps the lesson of most crucial importance my dad gave me was developing a strong work ethic. It constantly guides all my endeavors. These are things I will carry with me for the rest of my life."

Chelsea Nun, Age 20

"For me, Dad's Class was something that I grew up with; it was something that I expected. But as I got older, I realized that it wasn't as common as I had made it out to be. Things like balancing a check book, taking out a loan, or learning about car insurance were things about which my friends had no idea. Dad's Class has better prepared me for life and taught me things that I couldn't learn in school, things that mattered. Not only that, it has also created a better, healthier relationship with my own dad, which is something that a lot of people I know haven't truly experienced."

Bri Nun, Age 18

"Through Dad's Class, I have gained understanding and practical skills needed for a successful future. I have been given the opportunity to learn from my dad's life experiences and wisdom. Dad's Class has also been a chance for my dad and I to spend time together and develop a deeper relationship."

Lauren Nun, Age 16

DAD'S CLASS

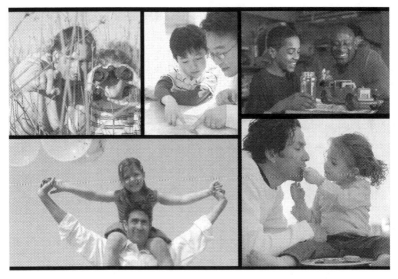

INTERACTING · CONNECTING · MENTORING

DENNIS L. NUN

WestBow Press books may be ordered through booksellers or by contacting:

WestBow Press
A Division of Thomas Nelson
1663 Liberty Drive
Bloomington, IN 47403
www.westbowpress.com
1-(866) 928-1240

Because of the dynamic nature of the Internet, any Web addresses or links contained in this book may have changed since publication and may no longer be valid. The views expressed in this work are solely those of the author and do not necessarily reflect the views of the publisher, and the publisher hereby disclaims any responsibility for them.

ISBN: 978-1-4497-0237-3 (sc)
ISBN: 978-1-4497-0238-0 (hc)
ISBN: 978-1-4497-0236-6 (e)

Library of Congress Control Number: 2010929962

Printed in the United States of America

WestBow Press rev. date: 6/3/2010

DAD'S
CLASS

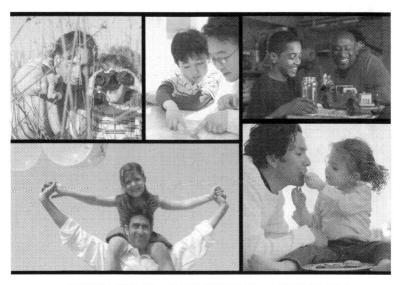

INTERACTING · CONNECTING · MENTORING

DENNIS L. NUN

Table of Contents

Introduction: Growing Up With Dad's Class   17

by Sarah Nun

Chapter 1: What Is Dad's Class?   25

Chapter 2: Dad's Class Rules   37

Chapter 3: What Should We Talk About?   71

Chapter 4: Stewardship: *It's A Material World*   83

Chapter 5: Relationships: *Dealing with People*   113

Chapter 6: Confidence: *Personal Development*   133

Chapter 7: Faith: *Wisdom, Spiritual Truth,*

and Philosophy   171

Chapter 8: Dads: *The Good, The Bad, and The Ugly*   185

Appendix:

    Suggested Reading   198

    Your Story   202

    Acknowledgments   207

    About the Author   208

Dedicated to my wife, Patty

*who blessed me with six wonderful children
and then allowed me to spend time
with each of them, encouraging them
to become all they could be in Christ.*

Introduction

Growing Up With Dad's Class

by Sarah Nun

I have to admit, I was mostly interested in the food. Or at least, my young mind came to associate bowls of honey-crusted granola and tall glasses of chocolate milk with the regular breakfast outings my father and I shared. Even as a young child I was the antithesis of a morning person, and it was in a confused daze that my mom would wrestle me from sleep, comb my hair, and bundle me up to go out for breakfast. It wasn't until I was standing outside in the morning cold that I'd realize I was no longer in bed. I'd look up at my father grinning at me from under his wide cowboy hat, thundering of Stetson cologne, and I knew something was special about the day.

While we waited at the restaurant for our breakfast, my dad and I would draw pictures on our napkins. He would let me look through his planner and patiently answer my obscure questions like, "How do batteries work?" or "Why do fingers get wrinkly in the bathtub?" As I grew up, our breakfast conversations did also. Throughout junior high and high school, conversations evolved to planning for college, applying for jobs, and managing finances. My dad taught me to set goals, to be dedicated in my work, and to be a woman of my word. He taught me these things not only though Dad's Class lessons, but also through the way he lived his life.

In my adult years, I've been stunned by how many of my peers don't understand the basics of holding down a job or managing finances. When I encounter people who are "in the dark" about such things, I have to admit my initial reaction is "Didn't you learn that in Dad's Class?" But not everyone did. It's an odd sort of blind-sightedness that we assume our experiences are typical. But what else does a child know, after all? I thought all dads wore cowboy hats and Stetson cologne. I thought all dads took their kids on breakfast dates and had thoughtful, caring talks over long car rides. I didn't understand that some kids didn't even know their fathers; or that some dads, although physically present in their homes, were emotionally absent.

When I was eighteen, I moved away to college. Looking back now, I'm surprised I had the courage to start a new life on my own in a place where I knew no one. But I also see how well my parents, my father in particular, prepared me for the transition. All along, he'd been telling me I had potential and could accomplish the things I set my mind to. By the time I had to face the "real world" and the discouraging messages it sent my way, the encouraging voice of my father was well-rooted and gave me the confidence to persevere.

College is an intense intersection of childhood and adulthood that gives one ample time to think about both. As I settled into college life and made new friends, it became apparent that as young adults we carry much of our childhood with us. In the midst of selecting majors, pulling all-nighters, and selling our souls to any number of campus associations, we were also struggling with deeper issues. Many late night heart-to-heart conversations with friends revealed that nearly everyone I knew was dealing with dad issues. I remember hearing only a few stories of evil abusive fathers, but I remember countless tales of paternal neglect—heartbreaking accounts of children who reached out to their fathers for love and affirmation, only to be confronted by a man too afraid to say he loved them. I couldn't believe how few of my friends even talked to their fathers on a regular basis; many people confessed they had seldom, if ever, experienced a meaningful father-child conversation.

> *Many late night heart-to-heart conversations with friends revealed that nearly everyone I knew was dealing with dad issues.*

And then in graduate school, while pursuing my master's degree in sociology, I sat in a classroom of twenty-five feminists studying gender roles. I've always considered myself a Christian feminist, in large part because both of my parents made me feel empowered. My folks taught me that I could and should be an active player in the world, and I believed them. But I soon discovered I was, once again, in the minority.

Since the study of sociology of gender often turns toward discussions of family dynamics, I quickly learned the sense of empowerment I felt imparted to me by my parents was not shared by most of the students sitting in the classroom. When the discussion turned to the topic of fathers, student after student around the room confessed they either didn't know, didn't like, or no longer spoke to their father. When it was my turn to share, I was almost embarrassed to say I actually liked my dad. I told them I respect him and he respects me. I told them my parents had raised my brothers and sisters and I with the non-sexist mentality that we could accomplish great things. My monologue was followed by silence from the twenty-five feminists.

I realized in that moment that most of the people around me were dealing with a whole set of concerns that had never crossed my mind. Men and women in their twenties, thirties, and older, still torn up over the question of whether or not their dad loved them. I called up my dad after class and told him, "I just realized that along with all the other challenges we have to deal with as we're learning to be grown-ups in the big bad world, most of the people around me are also trying to figure out if their dad loves them. I had no idea how easy I have it."

I think what I am supposed to say at this point is that no matter how terrible of a father you've been, you can make it right. But I think deep down we all know that isn't true. It's probably accurate to say you can make things *better*, and I would encourage any father at any point along the way to strive to do so. If there is a rift between you and your grown child, it's definitely worth making a phone call to begin the process of healing. But the reality is if you miss your child's formative years, you are likely to miss the opportunity to really know him or her. While you can certainly plan for a better future, you can never go back and retrieve those magical years of childhood.

As we grow older we train our hearts to be more logical and resilient, but to a child everything is monumental. To this day I am convinced I will never again drink a bigger glass of chocolate milk than I had at breakfast with my dad when I was four years old. And if I knew then that my dad loved me and had time for me, it's a lot easier to be convinced the same is true now as an adult.

The fact that my father is writing this book about parenting, and the fact that I just spent the last few pages bragging on him, probably makes my family sound like a pretty perfect bunch. But let me assure you, none of us is perfect, and that includes my dad. In fact, sometimes he can be pretty annoying. Take, for example, an experience I had in college when I came home on a break and told him my car shook uncontrollably as I drove it. I said I was concerned this might be a problem and that I was losing friends because people were afraid to ride with me. He would respond in his nauseatingly optimistic way, "Oh, it never shakes when I drive it. I think it's fine." He denied anything was wrong with the car until the day it was towed out of the parking lot and sold for parts.

And there are many things—things of far more significance than an aging Volvo that my dad and I have disagreed on over the years. But along with the lessons my dad taught me about finances and work ethic, he also taught me (and showed me) that people aren't perfect, but we love each other

> *It's amazing how if you talk to your kids about how to balance a checkbook or apply for a job, they'll be much more likely to come talk to you about more significant crossroads in their lives.*

anyway. Your spouse may be driving you crazy, but you still come home at the end of the day. Family fights escalate, but when the storm has passed you come back to each other with "I'm sorry" and "I love you." I was never under the impression that I had perfect parents (and I'm certain that at times, they felt the same about me), but I was assured perfection was not a qualification for love.

Much has changed in my life since the days when my biggest concern was wrinkly fingers in the bathtub, but the relationship my father built with me as a child has in many ways remained the same. It's amazing how if you talk to your kids about how to balance a checkbook or apply for a job, they'll be much more likely to come talk to you about more significant crossroads in their lives.

This book can be summed up in one sentence: *Spend time with your kids.* And while you're at it, teach 'em some stuff. But even before you teach, try listening. You'll be surprised what your kids share when they know they have the loving attention of their dad.

I only have one complaint: *Why'd we have to have Dad's Class in the morning? So . . . early . . . in . . . the . . . morning!*

CHAPTER 1

What Is Dad's Class?

Defining Dad's Class

The only thing that qualifies me to write a book about parenting is that I am a dad who desperately loves his children and wants them to be prepared for their future with the knowledge that they are loved. Dad's Class was born out of my desire to be the best dad I could be, intentionally equipping my sons and daughters the best that I could to meet the challenges of their adult lives.

I'm not a perfect dad. Patty's not a perfect mom. As much as we might like to think so, our kids aren't perfect kids. We recognize that our church and Christian school have come alongside Patty and I to encourage our children to understand God's world in the light of His Word. Their continual support and the consistent message delivered in words and in lives modeled before them has been a blessing. The teachers, preachers, administrators, coaches and mentors who have influenced our children haven't been perfect, however. We're all fallen people in a fallen world. Even in our home, we've experienced and witnessed the trauma and drama of real life. That is exactly why I want to do the best I can to counter the immoral gravity that is all around us, encouraging our kids to see the world as it really is and dealing with life as it comes at them.

Over the years I've stressed to the kids that Dad's Class is really "a life-long seminar in applied wisdom." My advice to each of my children has been this consistent message: "In life you will have enough trials without creating more for yourself by making one—or a series of bad decisions." The foundation of my advice to them is, "Seek wisdom. Avoid fools."

It's been said that anyone can be a father, but it takes a special person to be a dad. In my case it wasn't that easy, which was probably a blessing, as it turned out.

Patty and I were married in 1973. While we didn't plan on starting our family right away, when we decided to move into the child bearing years, achieving a pregnancy turned out to be one of the greatest challenges of our lives. We spent five intense years and mountains of money, working with obstetricians and fertility specialists, and then with adoption agencies in the hope of starting a family. The other couples we met in the lengthy adoption process had all received a baby. We were still waiting.

> *Dad's Class is really "a life-long seminar in applied wisdom."*

While the investment of our time and resources spent trying to have our first child were significant, the emotional struggles were the greater challenge. We prayed and cried on a regular basis. I know that it was the hardest on Patty. I felt helpless trying to heal her broken heart, as she longed to hold a baby of her own. She wanted a child so badly, but God was denying that desire. One day, during a time of prayer, we asked God specifically, not to give us children *unless they would grow up to love Him and love each other.*

Resigning ourselves to the idea that God may have other plans for us, there was a new sense of peace. Not long after that, we half-heartedly decided to seek one more medical opinion. We were referred to Dr. Thomas Hilgers, who turned out to be an internationally known infertility specialist. He figured out pretty quickly the multifaceted causes of our problems from a biological and reproductive perspective. Following another lengthy surgery and one more miscarriage, we found ourselves expecting our first child. Sarah Elizabeth Nun was born in the spring of 1982, followed by brothers Adam Joseph and Jordan David and sisters Chelsea Catherine, Brianna Grace and Lauren Danielle. Six healthy children in eleven years put us well into the parenting years, and we were loving every minute of it.

We were blessed with a church family that supported

us through those years of challenge. In fact, we counted over 125 baby gifts that came from people all over the country who had been praying along with us for the birth of Sarah. We were also blessed with a business that allowed us to spend lots of time as a family at home and on the road. We listened intently to the advice of other parents and took advantage of all the parenting radio programs, videos and books that Dr. Dobson put out from Focus on the Family. We also observed the successes and failures that we saw taking place in families all around us.

From the time Sarah was born, I had the desire to be a dad who loved my wife and was actively involved in encouraging and nurturing my children. Perhaps it was due to the long and painful wait we endured, that I felt a special appreciation for these new lives God had entrusted to us. Maybe my motivation was the result of what I felt my own family had offered me as well as a painful recognition of those things it lacked during my growing-up years. While my years as a child were stable in most ways, I was left hoping that I could offer even more to my kids during their formative years.

Growing up on a farm in Nebraska, I had the opportunity to spend day and night working and learning alongside my father and mother (who was also a teacher). We raised and harvested a variety of crops. I drove the tractor and tended to the chickens, hogs, sheep, goats, horses and cattle. There were always dogs and cats to play with and you could hunt, fish, ride your bike, take part in a 4-H club meeting or go camping. Our church was a key part of our community and our life, as well.

Both sets of my grandparents lived about a mile away on their farms. I had what today is the rare opportunity to spend lots of time with both sets of grandparents, along with aunts, uncles and cousins. Included in my family was my Great Grandpa Nedza, who came over from Poland when he was just a young man. I really enjoyed that dimension of my early life. Dad and Mom were intelligent people, worked hard and loved each other. If there was one thing I lacked, it was the direct counsel and advice that I'd always sought—especially from my father.

I knew that raising my kids in the city wouldn't be the same. When they got older I knew that they'd be able to go with me on some of my out-of-town, out-of-state, or even international business trips. An occasional trip with dad wasn't going to be a substitute for the daily one-on-one time that I'd enjoyed with my dad and mom growing up, especially during the pre-school and elementary school years. So, being pragmatic, I wanted to be intentional about setting aside time I could spend with each of them individually. My initial plan was to take each of the kids out on a date weekly, even if for just an errand or to get a coke. As they got older and busier, the dates were more like once a month, but more intentional and longer.

When Sarah was no more than a year old, Patty encouraged me to start taking her on dates. Mom would get Sarah dressed and then we'd head off to one of our favorite restaurants. Those early dates were more an opportunity for mom to get some rest or do something on her own. (She was already pregnant with Adam when Sarah was just 9 months old.) These dates were also an opportunity for me to show off my daughter, and they set the stage for what we later began calling *Dad's Class*.

In order to encourage the kids to remember the topics we discussed in Dad's Class and to write down some thoughts of their own, I bought each of them a journal. The topics were wide and varied, and until being asked to write this book, I never really had any organization to the ideas and concepts that we discussed.

First and foremost, I wanted us to just enjoy spending time together. Sometimes I'd do most of the talking. At other times all I would do is listen and ask a few leading questions. I recognized that even with the exposure they each had to great Bible teaching and the wisdom of Scripture at church and school, there were practical topics that just got overlooked. These were things that you really need to know when you get out into the world like:

- *How to open a checking account and keep it balanced*
- *How and why we buy insurance*
- *How to buy a house*
- *What's the difference between an appreciating and a depreciating asset?*
- *How to tithe and save and why*
- *How to get a job and why*
- *How to be successful in life, and how you define "success"*
- *How to be a good steward*
- *How to build a great reputation you can be proud of*
- *How to win friends*
- *How to manage your time*
- *How to make the hard decisions*
- *How to recognize and make the most of your talents and abilities*
- *How to ask really great questions and why they're so important*
- *How to develop good habits*
- *What's bad about tobacco, alcohol and drugs?*
- *What's the difference between knowledge and wisdom?*
- *Why and how do we pay taxes?*
- *Why we serve others*
- *What's wrong with sex outside of marriage?*
- *What is a "life philosophy" and how do we develop reality-based philosophies that work?*

These and dozens of other topics I've included in the pages of this book make for great discussion points with kids as they grow into what we hope them to be: mature, stable, productive adults.

Taking on these topics and discussing them openly and intelligently is what Dad's Class is all about. I'm no rocket scientist, but I know that every dad alive has experiences and wisdom to share with his children. That's why the original design was for both a father and mother to provide the biological requirements necessary to birth a new life, and then together provide for the spiritual, educational and psychological needs of that child.

> *Every dad has experiences and wisdom to share with his children.*

The objective is to take the raw material with which our babies arrive on this earth and gradually to mold it into mature, responsible, and God-fearing adults.

James Dobson

What you will find in the pages of *Dad's Class* are eight rules that include:

- Rule I: Don't prejudge the value of time spent with your child.
- Rule II: The best time to start Dad's Class is NOW.
- Rule III: Seek the assistance of others. Develop a support system.
- Rule IV: Begin with Show and Tell and ask questions.
- Rule V: Make Dad's Class age and child appropriate.
- Rule VI: Take some notes.
- Rule VII: Develop a system that works for you and encourages them.
- Rule VIII: Don't allow yourself to get discouraged.

Following these basic rules I'll share with you a sampling of over 60 topics and dozens of questions to launch your own personalized version of Dad's Class.

What I discovered, by accident, in the process of leading my kids in our Dad's Class sessions, is how different each child's personality was expressed when they

> *There is nothing more important to your son or daughter than your undivided attention.*

were all alone with me, out of the shadow of sibling rivalry and the noise of our family's home life. The family times were great during those growing up years and they continue to be. However, it is the individual times I've enjoyed with each of my children that are priceless. Without these times, I know that my relationships with each of them would not be what it is today; and I would never have gotten to know them as the individuals they are, with their unique personalities, gifts and talents. The depth and intensity of our relationships and the open communication that has resulted, have returned to us any investment of time and resources hundreds of times over.

I've heard it said that the job of a leader is *to define reality as it is and then bring together the resources to deal with that reality.* There is a desperate need today for godly, fatherly leadership in our homes. It's up to us as dads to deliver that leadership.

I want to encourage any dad who is taking the time to read Dad's Class, that there is nothing more important to your son or daughter than your undivided attention. I highly recommend the intentional investment of time and effort to give your children the undivided attention they deserve and long for. And while you are spending that time together, these pages just might give you some ideas and concepts worth talking about.

Each child is unique, a special creation of God with talents, abilities, personality, preference, dislikes, potentials, strengths, weaknesses, and skills that are his or her own. As parents, we must seek to identify these in each of our children and help them become the persons God intended.

Dave Veerman

CHAPTER 2

Dad's Class Rules

There is a story about an old man who was going through his attic one day and came across a journal that was his son's when he was very young. He'd never seen the journal before and didn't even know his son had kept one. As he looked at the dates in the journal and read some of the entries, he quickly ascertained that his son had been nine years old at the time.

He read through a few of the entries and realized how fast his children had grown up, how busy it was back in those days and how hard he had worked to support them for so many years. With his wife gone now, and the kids each living several states away, he realized how much he missed them all and how lonely his life had become.

For years he'd kept a day planner of his daily business activities, and he thought it would be interesting to compare his calendar entries with those of his nine-year-old son. He took the journal back to his study and pulled his old planner from his file cabinet for that particular year and laid it out on his desk. As he paged through his calendar he noted one particular date; June 15th, a Saturday. His notes read, "Took Tommy fishing. Didn't catch a thing. Wasted a day." He opened up Tommy's journal to

June 15th and read these words: "Went fishing with Dad today. The BEST DAY OF MY LIFE!"

In his book *The 7 Secrets of Effective Fathers*, Dr. Ken Canfield, founder of the National Center for Fathering, relates the conclusion of years of statistical research on what effective fathers do that others don't do. Beginning with the basic assumptions that fathering is important; it is a learned skill; and it brings with it great rewards, he goes on to relate the seven things that stand out about the most effective fathers:

1. They demonstrate long-term **commitment** to their children and spouse.
2. They **know their children**.
3. They are **consistent**, meaning regular, predictable and dependable.
4. They accept the role of **protector and provider** for their family.
5. They **love their spouse** and demonstrate it in front of their children.
6. They **actively listen** to their family.
7. They **equip their children spiritually** to develop a faith of their own.

Dad's Class is nothing more than a platform for you to work toward developing the skills and relationships with each of your children that give them the most loving and secure environment possible, to discover who they are and what they can become.

I'm not very big on rules. In fact, I identify with the old adage that "Rules are made to be broken." However, here are some rules to guide you, if you'd like to begin conducting a Dad's Class with your son or daughter.

Rule I
DON'T PREJUDGE THE VALUE
OF TIME SPENT WITH YOUR CHILD.

If I were to dictate an overarching rule for your version of Dad's Class, it would have to begin here: It's all about making the effort to spend one-on-one time with your child. We've all heard that love is spelled T-I-M-E, and it really is.

Our kids, whether they are 2, 12, 32, or 62, want to know they're important to us. They may not say it, but the thought that goes through every kid's head is this: *If I were important to Dad, he'd have time for me. Everything else and everyone else seem more important to him.*

In fact, if you really want to make it clear to them that this is time set aside just for them, ditch the cell phone. Let your wife know where you are in case of emergency, but be unavailable to everyone else. **This is your special**

time with a very special person in your life. You won't believe how just knowing that will set the stage for great times with your son or daughter.

I would argue that there is no single person in anyone's life from whom they need affirmation more than from their father. Not that our mothers aren't equally important to nurture us, but it comes more naturally for mom. She carried you for nine months. In most cases she cared for you, fed you, and rocked you for the first years of your life. She's the one who took care of you when dad was at work and perhaps when you came home from school, if you were lucky.

Dads, because of their very nature and frequent absences, are typically less nurturing. That is precisely the reason we need to work at it. Because when we do provide just a little affirmation, time and attention, it goes a long way toward encouraging our children. They feel special when dad is at that ball game, dance recital, swimming lesson, track meet or band concert. They may act cool and unimpressed, but did you catch them glancing at you out of the corner of their eye? It *does matter* to them that you made time for them, even if they don't tell you so.

Any attempt you make to spend time with your children is a move in the right direction—as long as you don't do something stupid, like spending that time being critical, sarcastic, or angry. In fact, the more you do just the opposite—by showing and telling them how much you love, respect, appreciate and take pride in them—the more they will look forward to these times together. **Whatever activity you had planned or whatever topic you expected to talk about isn't nearly as important as just spending time getting to know them one-on-one, listening to, and encouraging them.**

Educator Samuel Sava said, *"It's not better teachers, texts or curricula that our children need most; it's better childhoods, and we will never see lasting school reform until we see parent reform."* We can do better, and it begins with setting aside the time for them.

Rule II
THE BEST TIME TO START
DAD'S CLASS IS NOW.

The best time to plant a tree was 20 years ago.
The second best time is today.

Regardless of the age of your children, **right now** is the best time to begin scheduling regular time to interact with them individually. The younger they are, the better. They'll be receptive to just about anything you want to do early on.

The older your children are, and the less time you've made for them in the past, the more challenging it will be to adjust to your desire to spend time with them. And if they are into the teenage years or older, they are at a busy time in their lives. Your window is closing. It's not shut, but it will definitely be more difficult for them to find time for you in the teens and beyond.

You'll need to be more creative as your children mature. I found it especially difficult to find time for Dad's Class as my kids started driving. One system we put into place was to offer **free gas with every Dad's Class**. Here's how it works at our house. If your car is running low on gas, you have two choices: fill it up yourself out of your own pocket, or set up a Dad's Class appointment and he'll fill 'er up! With today's gas prices, it's a pretty good incentive to make time for Dad.

Let me share with you some great advice that came from my friend and father of four grown children, Ben Welch. Ben said to me one day, when I was acting a little stressed about how fast my family was growing up, "Dennis, you're always going to be their dad. I spend as much time now with my adult children as I did with them when they were growing up." Hearing that was a breath of fresh air, and a real encouragement that I've never forgotten. I realized at that point that the real benefit of getting to know and enjoy my children as individuals now is that **I am laying the foundation for a life-long relationship to enjoy as they become adults.** I've already seen the reality of that with my older children who are now independent adults. I'm very proud of them and love to spend time with them whenever possible.

Each of your children is unique in his or her appearance, gifts, talents, personality and bents. You can be assured of just one thing: God doesn't make mistakes. He has given you the opportunity to shepherd your children and bring them up in the "nurture and admonition of the Lord" (Ephesians 6:4). Consider that God just may have given them the exact mix of traits that they possess to bring out the very best in you.

Our children have dramatically different personalities that I never would have discovered if I had not spent time with each of them individually.

Sarah is disciplined, organized, spiritual and loves to study, learn and have deep conversations. Being the big sister to all of the other Nuns that came along caused her to develop a responsibility that matured her far beyond her years. At seven, when she walked through the mall with Patty, people thought she was carrying a dolly. It was her sister Chelsea.

Adam is the musical, dramatic, creative, social grasshopper. He has always loved to read and often I would go to wake him in the morning to find the lamp glaring in his face, glasses still on, and a book beside him. Friends were always calling, wanting to know if he could come over to play or come to their birthday party.

Jordan is always trying new things. There were new pets all the time, exploration in the backyard that led to a scouting interest, that led to Eagle Scout. We would find him going through the refrigerator, looking for cucumbers or tomatoes that he would cut up and display on a plate and go door to door in the neighborhood, offering them for sale. Later he found a candy wholesaler and would buy large bags of candy, bring them home and offer for sale at retail prices to his siblings and neighborhood kids.

Chelsea is a beautiful, sweet, quiet young woman with all those natural blond curls that everyone wanted to touch. More than once (I hate to admit it) we'd be at a restaurant with the family or a group of friends and she'd ask "Am I going to get anything to eat?" We'd forget to order for her and she was too polite and quiet to get our attention. She's athletic, musical, and a great writer.

Bri is our performer, singing as long as I can remember. She's always loved music, drama, fashion and being all girl. While she loves to perform and is very gifted in music and drama, she has an eye for fashion and is an expert at finding a deal when shopping. She is set on being a fashion journalist or stylist.

Lauren is an intense distance athlete, basketball player, drummer, and the term "serious student" wouldn't come close to describing the energy she throws into everything she does. She may be the "baby" of the family, but she's as determined as they come.

We are proud of every one of the children God has blessed us with, and do our best to model Christ-like character. But when we don't—we say something mean or get into an argument—we try to be quick to mend fences. We use those vital words, *"I am sorry"*; and ask that crucial question, *"Can you forgive me?"*

Rule III
SEEK THE ASSISTANCE OF OTHERS.
DEVELOP A SUPPORT SYSTEM.

Successful parents recognize the need for an effective support system. My wife has always encouraged to me to spend personal time with the kids through Dad's Class, ski trips, fishing trips, going to concerts, or taking them on business trips. Patty and I also work hard at being on the same page with discipline and expectations for appropriate behavior from our kids. We try to discuss and resolve differences in private, not in front of the kids.

During the years of infertility and adoption applications, Patty and I had more time than most to think about the type of parents we wanted to be. Then when our family started to grow rapidly, we realized how overwhelming the task of parenting could be. Patty is the creative one in our family and not only encouraged me as I began the process of developing my Dad's Class routine, but also came up with other parenting systems as well.

One that she initiated was what we just call "days." With six kids eleven and younger, we began to systematically pray for one another each day. On Monday, everyone in the family would pray specifically for Sarah, our oldest. Tuesday was the day to pray for Adam. Wednesday we all prayed for Jordan. On Thursday, Friday and

Saturday we would pray for Chelsea, Bri and Lauren, respectively. On Sunday, everyone would pray for Mom and Dad. On his or her special "day" that child would pray specifically for Mom and Dad. We still encourage the kids to follow Mom's daily pattern of prayer that we began many years ago—no matter where we are in the world today. On Mondays we still pray for Sarah and know that she's praying for Mom and Dad on her "day" too.

In addition, Patty came up with a system called "weeks" to deal with the challenges of having six kids in the house. Each child would be assigned a week, in rotation. During their week, they would have specific duties and privileges. The person of the week would be responsible for:

- Taking out the trash.
- Helping mom cook dinner each evening.
- Clearing the table and washing dishes after dinner.

They would also have the following privileges:

- Answering the phone for the family (and Mom made sure they answered properly).
- Sitting in the front seat of the van whenever Mom drove (once they reached the legal height and weight minimums for front seat passengers).

- Going grocery shopping with Mom and picking out food they wanted to have at home.
- Picking out where we would eat Sunday dinner.
- Going out on a date during their week with Mom.

Patty and I developed other systems as well. By 7th grade, we taught our children:

- How to wash their own laundry.
- How to put themselves to bed *early enough to get themselves up on time.* (They no longer had an enforced bedtime going into 7th grade.) I have to admit, some of them developed this habit better and faster than others.
- The importance of serving others less fortunate through missions, outreach, and community service. During junior high (or no later than early high school years) we would begin looking for a mission trip for each of the kids to go on with our church. For over ten years our family has gone annually with a team sent out by our church to Ensenada, Mexico. In that community we have developed a relationship with a local church and ministry base. This was their first taste of foreign missions. From there they have gone to India, Bolivia, Brazil

and Venezuela. The kids raised their own funds to serve on these teams. We've also worked at a rescue mission, conducted a neighborhood vacation Bible school in a city park, led Bible studies in the local prison and taught in a small seminary.

- The importance of their spiritual heritage, by taking a trip to Israel. Sarah and Adam went with Patty when they were 12 and 13, Jordan went with me when he was 13. We took Chelsea to Israel before she reported to college and Bri and Lauren are looking forward to their trips. Given the challenges and cost of travel, there are many alternatives to actually traveling. If cost is prohibitive, try trips closer to home that focus on the heritage of your family or faith.

- The importance of relationship with Mom and Dad. At age 13, the boys would go on a trip with Dad and the girls a trip with Mom. Jordan went with me on a business trip to Europe and Israel, while Adam and I spent a week "road-tripping" and fishing in Canada. At the time when each of our daughters reached woman-hood, Patty would have a special trip with each of the girls and I would present them with a rose and dinner-date to mark this special milestone.

- The importance of purity. At age 13, I would take each of the girls on a very special date where I read to them a letter that I write just for them. It told them how much I loved them and appreciated the very special person they were. At the same time I would present them with a "purity necklace" that came with a key, which I kept and plan to give to their husband on the day of their wedding. We talked specifically about the importance of purity until marriage, a subject I also addressed with the boys at 13.

Patty and I recognized early on that even as fully engaged parents, our church and school needed to be strong positive influences that support our family values. The home, church, and school really work together like a three-legged stool providing a solid foundation for raising well-adjusted kids. The more consistent the message that these three institutions deliver, the less confusion our kids encounter in their growing-up years. We didn't have time to spend un-doing anything that our school or church was teaching or the bad influences that might be present there. We were blessed with a great Christian school that made our choice pretty simple. It was not without financial sacrifice, which we saw as an important investment in the raising of our children. For others, home school and their home school associations fill that need.

I realize not everyone has a support system with a present and encouraging spouse, a Christian school, and a solid church with an active youth group. There are single dads like my friend Mark Schulz, whose wife Jodi died young, leaving him alone to raise two young boys. Another friend Mark Schwarting, survived the pain of divorce and was given full custody of his three teenage boys. I know single moms trying to be both father and mother to their kids. I am moved when I see the burden under which these parents labor to be a positive influence on their children.

Whatever your situation, get help from your church, school, or other resources (such as the Boy Scouts or Girl Scouts) that might be available in your area. Parenting is too big a job to be done solo.

IF THE MARRIAGE IS BROKEN, THE KIDS DON'T NEED TO BE

Divorce, while unfortunate, is a fact of life for millions of families. So what should you do if you're a divorced dad? Well, the answer is both straightforward and simple: You must do whatever it takes to stay totally involved with your kids.

Sadly, far too many dads go missing in action after their divorce. They may provide financial support and then suppose that their parenting responsibilities have been fulfilled. But of course, nothing could be further from the truth.

Children of divorced parents need heaping helpings of support, for obvious reasons. So if you're a divorced father, don't let anything or anybody deter you from your parental responsibilities. Your children need you now, perhaps more than ever.

If you are married to the mother of your children, then the first step in developing a healthy relationship with your kids is to love your wife. You are demonstrating, through your marriage relationship the kind of person you are, and the kind of person you would like them to become. Treating their mother well by being loving, patient, and respectful will be a strong example that will impact their view of what a healthy marriage should be.

I've heard it said that if you want to know what type of husband a young man will be, look at his father. And if you want to know what type of wife a girl will be, look at her mother. That's often a very accurate indicator. As parents we need to ask ourselves, "Are we modeling the type of men and women, husbands and wives we want our children to be as adults?" For the sake of your children, love their mom. Date her too. A strong marriage is the best foundation on which to build a family with effective parenting.

Rule IV
BEGIN WITH SHOW AND TELL AND ASK QUESTIONS.

In my work, I get an opportunity to attend and conduct sales and management training programs. I've utilized a number of training tools and techniques over the years, some of which are pretty high tech. The conclusion I've come to is that the best universal method of learning is what we did in kindergarten class: *Show and Tell.* We all enjoy hearing and telling stories. If the teller has a prop that relates to the story he's telling, it is even better!

The best stories that you can tell are about experiences that have made you into the person that you are today. Our kids don't know what it was like to grow up without computers, the internet, YouTube, flat-screens, HDTV, XBox, Facebook, Twitter, iPods and iPhones. There are funny stories, sad stories, embarrassing stories, tragic stories, and scary stories about what your life was like growing up in the olden days. Some of the stories about you, your parents, and your grandparents they'll never know unless you take the time to tell them. Our children might gain an enhanced appreciation for their dad once they understand more about where he's come from, versus just seeing him where he is today.

Remember, the details are what make any story interesting. Cultivate and develop your story-telling abilities. You might be surprised at how interested your children are in the tales of your childhood. Some of your stories they will want to hear over and over again.

Our children have stories that are important for them to tell too. We need to listen. They might be going through challenging times that seem insurmountable to them. **They need you to listen to them** or they may find someone else who will. Dad's Class, more than anything else, serves to let your son or daughter know that you are available to hear the stories that describe what is going on in their lives.

An important part of the conversations you have will be the time you spend getting them to talk. This is something that can be difficult for some kids, especially at particular stages of adolescence. In sales communication, we teach that effective sales professionals will spend 80 percent of their time listening and 20 percent of their time talking. That 20 percent of the time spent talking should be spent *asking the right questions*. Learn to ask, sincere, probing, intelligent questions. As a counselor, Patty would say they need to be "open-ended" questions—ones that can't be answered with a yes or no. Examples of these kinds of conversation starters would be questions like these:

Describe your day to me.
Tell me some more about that.
How did that make you feel?
What did that make you want to do?
What did you think when that happened?

You will be teaching some important skills just by modeling them in Dad's Class. How to be a good listener, communicator, storyteller and conversationalist will serve your children for a lifetime. Do it well and you'll enjoy the results for the rest of your life, as your children grow into mature adults. How do you feel when someone takes the time to listen to you?

I've learned that people will forget what you said,
people will forget what you did, but people
will never forget how you made them feel.
Maya Angelou

Rule V
MAKE DAD'S CLASS AGE
AND CHILD APPROPRIATE.

The younger you start a routine of Dad's Class with your kids, the easier it is to schedule, and the more anxious they are to hear what you have to share. Setting a regular schedule or building your meeting time around a specific activity, helps make it consistent.

When he was very young, my son Adam and I would go to a weekly prayer breakfast on Saturday mornings and then go out together afterward. He looked forward to the breakfast and that big glass of chocolate milk, as much as our conversations. My son Jordan was involved in Boy Scouts, and I went with him to most meetings and campouts. It gave us additional time to spend together that served as Dad's Class appointments.

With Chelsea and Lauren, basketball and cross-country events are good times for Dad's Class appointments. With Bri, it has been music lessons and drama for the most part. When children are younger, you'll have more ability to set the schedule and give direction to the activities. As they get older, friends and activities more often dictate the schedule, meaning you'll need to be more creative and flexible.

The topics I suggest are just starting points for

discussions that provide practical information they'll need as adults. There is one thing that I've realized over the years: **our kids can understand a lot more at a young age, than most of us would like to admit.** We set the stage and demonstrate that we view them as intelligent, maturing individuals, ready to discuss challenging ideas and concepts

Mark Brandenburg in his list of "Top Ten Ways to be a Better Father" (www.christianfathers.com) leads off his list with *seeing your kids as capable.* If we give our kids the impression that they're not good enough and can't live up to our standards—even subconsciously—they will sense it. The more approval, encouragement, and pride we take in them, the more they will strive to reach to our expectations. If we talk to them about important "adult topics" and treat them with respect, they often exceed our expectations in the mature ways in which they respond to the discussion.

When my son Jordan was just eight, we were talking about the power of compound interest and principles of stewardship. We even got him a Crown Financial ABC Bank (www.crown.org) with compartments for tithing, saving and spending, as a visual reminder of the lesson.

Whatever the topic, it is important to talk in terms they can understand. At age 16, a teenager is about to get his driver's license and usually motivated to talk about what goes into owning a car. There are car ownership expenses that most kids don't think about. It's not just the price of the vehicle (as adults have learned), but the ongoing expenses of gas, oil, maintenance, insurance, tires, registration, license plates, and taxes. Make it interesting. It's like any message that's worth telling: *it needs to be told in an interesting way.*

SONS AND DAUGHTERS HAVE DIFFERENT NEEDS.

Whether your child is son or daughter or you are blessed with both, you learn early on that boys and girls very have different needs. Of course each child is unique, but there tend to be specific bents and needs for each gender. Boys tend to be more rough and tumble, and need the physical activity that only a father figure can provide. Whether it is playing catch, going fishing, going camping or to a ball game, they tend to be more activity oriented.

This comes easier to dads, but we need to remember that our sons need us to model how to be gentle and willing to talk about needs and feelings with them as well. They need to be taught that it is alright for a man to show emotions, affection, and appreciation. They need us to demonstrate respect for their mother and other females in their life. Holding the door and demonstrating good manners are best learned from a dad.

Our daughters on the other hand, need to learn what to expect from a man who honors, respects, and cherishes them. We provide that model by listening, being patient, and demonstrating the level of respect they'll learn to expect from young men who come calling in the future. If you have daughters, be sure to get a copy of Robert Wolgemuth's book *She Calls Me Daddy.* My oldest daughter Sarah gave me a copy with the really important stuff highlighted, knowing that I have many years of parenting her three sisters to go. It is an excellent resource.

> *Find out what they like to do and integrate it into your time together.*

Rule VI
TAKE SOME NOTES.

Encourage them to write something down to help them remember what you talked about. Get them a journal that they keep just for your times together. They might keep it in their room or you might keep it. It doesn't make any difference how cryptic, misspelled or sloppy the notes are, this is a record of your time together more than anything else.

There will be times you get together when they don't really want to talk about the topic you'd planned to discuss. You won't always ask them to take notes. Sometimes the time together is purely recreational. That's all right. Be flexible and go with the flow. I said before, I've never had a real lesson plan. The most important thing is to spend time together getting to know your son or daughter. Remember rule #1? It's all about the T-I-M-E. I don't believe you can predict what will turn out to be "quality time." Just set aside the time and invest it with your child on faith.

What you talk about on any given day, and how you address it, will also depend upon the personality of the individual child. Find out what they like to do and integrate it into your time together. My boys like to go out to eat, take a road trip or work on something—at their home or ours—to get them in a conversational mood. My girls want to go to the coffee shop, a movie, or shopping. This is more about cultivating a relationship, which is a process—not an event. Learn to enjoy the time together and their individual personalities.

Rule VII
DEVELOP A SYSTEM THAT WORKS FOR YOU
AND ENCOURAGES THEM.

I remember the first time someone saw my planner and asked me, "Why do you have to have appointments on the calendar for Patty and the kids?" I made the statement that if I didn't intentionally set time aside to spend time with them, other things sometimes crowd them out of my calendar. I don't think they were very impressed, but for me it was a practical imperative. Scheduling family time into my weekly calendar is the assurance that my time with them will be protected. In order to reach the goals I have, I must plan how my time is going to be invested in my relationship with my wife and children, as well as in my work, Bible study, recreation, and community service.

I believe that any type of a Dad's Class that you decide to integrate into your schedule is going to have a positive impact on your relationship with your children. **As long as you have as an overall goal to spend this time with your children—getting to know, appreciate, and encourage them—it is destined to be a positive influence on their lives.** Because we know that the world, and many of the people in it, will not encourage and build up our kids, we need to work overtime to undo the negative impact that they (or we) may have had up to this point.

In his book *Words that Hurt, Words that Heal*, Rabbi Joseph Telushkin tells the story of a man who attended his wife's funeral:

> *After the service, everyone left the cemetery except for the mourning husband and the rabbi. The husband remained at the grave for a long while; finally, the rabbi approached him. "The service is long over, it is time for you to leave," he said.*
>
> *The man waved him away. "You don't understand. I loved my wife."*
> *"I am sure you did," the rabbi answered, "but you have been here a long time. You should go now."*
> *Again the husband said, "You don't understand. I loved my wife."*
> *Once more the rabbi urged him to leave.*
> *"But you don't understand," the man told him. "I loved my wife—and once, I almost told her."*

This story describes what Telushkin calls one of the most common and saddest human traits. He calls it *emotional constipation*, or an inability to express love, gratitude, and care when these emotions are felt. The people who suffer from this malady are not necessarily incapable of expressing all emotions; many are quite adept at sharing anger and annoyance. Only when gentler emotions are called for, do they become strangely reticent.

What others need from us on an ongoing basis, especially our children, is to know that they are cared for, that their good deeds inspire our gratitude, and that they are loved. It's that simple.

In his book, *Whale Done!*, Ken Blanchard addresses the importance of re-direction and recognition as teaching tools. He wrote this book with the help of trainers from SeaWorld, who train killer whales like Shamu to jump twenty feet out of their tank, to the amazement of their audiences. Ken says that there are really only four methods for managing people:

- **Ignore them.** This is not very effective, but very popular. Let people do whatever they want to do, and there's no telling what the results will be.
- **The "swoop and poop" seagull method.** You wait until you catch people doing something wrong, swoop in and squawk at them, leave your droppings and swoop out. This is very discouraging to people, and again is not very effective in getting people to do what you want them to do. Nevertheless, it is very popular.

- **Redirect them.** If you catch people doing things *almost* right, **encourage them in that direction with positive reinforcement and redirection.** This will allow them to feel good about themselves, look for progress, and appreciate your input.

- **Recognize them.** When you catch them doing things right, praise them and provide rewards. This is the ultimate tool for building self-confidence and giving people positive reinforcement.

The most frequently asked question of the trainers at SeaWorld is, "How do you get them to do that?" The answer is really very simple. With an animal as powerful as a killer whale, you cannot physically coerce it into submission. The trainer is forced to work within the nature of these giants of the sea to get them to consistently perform amazing feats.

What trainers do is totally centered on **redirection** and **recognition.** They place a rope across the middle of his pool, below the water but high enough that he can swim *over* or *under* the rope. When he swims underneath it, they totally ignore him. When he swims over it, he gets recognized with his favorite food. They keep raising the rope, continuing to ignore him when he swims underneath it but rewarding him for going over the rope. This continues until he's 20 feet out of the water and ready to perform for you and your family. Sound simple? It is.

People who are praised gain confidence. Your employees and your children will do the same. Redirection and recognition require an investment of time, but the result is a lot more positive than any of the alternatives. One more thing to remember: Always be sure to **praise in public but correct in private**.

Dad's Class gives you a platform for providing that encouragement, affirmation, and occasional redirection in a way that is natural, convenient and enjoyable for you and your son or daughter. If you choose not to use a journal, OK. If you decide not to use any of the topics that I suggest, fine. These things are not nearly as important as spending focused time in a private setting, appreciating your son or daughter for who they are and taking the time to tell them how proud you are of them. What you want them to sense from spending time with you is: **I like myself better when I'm with Dad**. If your system and time with your child produces that result, then you have succeeded in providing the confidence necessary for successful adult life. Encouragement instills confidence.

Rule VIII
DON'T LET YOURSELF
GET DISCOURAGED.

I have a lot of heros in my life. Many of them don't even know the impact they've had on me. One is Patrick John Hughes of Louisville, Kentucky. He is the proud father of Patrick Henry Hughes, born blind—without eyes, and with a crippling condition that prevents him from ever walking. In his words, Patrick's father says, "Countless dreams died. We were just devastated. We couldn't understand why."

But, when little Patrick was just less than one-year old, he began plunking away at the family piano and was soon able to duplicate what someone had played. By age two he was playing songs by request. Patrick's father said, "I felt that we weren't going to be able to play ball, but we were going to play music together."

Patrick's reputation as a pianist and a trumpet player proceeded him as he enrolled at the University of Louisville. Today he is a part of the 214 members of the Louisville Cardinals college marching band, his father pushing his wheel chair in formation with the other band members. Dad rolls and rotates the wheel chair, makes every practice, and sits with him in every class. How does he do it? He works the graveyard shift at UPS so that he's able to spend his days with his son at practices, attending classes and going to games.

I was blessed with six wonderful kids for whom we prayed long and hard, but who are healthy and bright. They are the highlight of my life. I tell them frequently how they make us look like much better parents than we really are. But, I can tell you that over the years I have had some really terrible Dad's Classes, where I got the silent treatment. Nothing I could say or do would produce anything other than a glaring stare or sarcastic remark. In some cases, I had said or done something to trigger that response. I deserved it.

> *We all have bad days and just about every relationship will go through ups and downs. Don't be discouraged. Think of it as a form of discipline, which James would say is "a testing of your faith."*

There was the time that my daughter was having the greatest trauma of her young life and I took a cell phone call. It was unforgivable.

There are days when nothing works and the bottom seems to fall out of your relationship. You really need to make amends, but either you can't or they won't hear it. That's when you begin to pray and remember 1 Thessalonians 3:4 which says, "and it came to pass…." It's a good day to remember Patrick John Hughes too and the sacrifices and challenges that others face—with a smile no less.

When those days happen, just remember: *it comes, but it will pass*. We all have bad days and just about every relationship will go through ups and downs. Don't be discouraged. Think of it as a form of discipline, which James would say is "a testing of your faith" (James 1:1-4) and remember that "all discipline for the moment seems not to be joyful, but sorrowful; yet to those who have been trained by it, afterwards it yields the peaceful fruit of righteousness" (Hebrews 12:11 NASB).

Try to figure out what went wrong, be ready to apologize and then move on. Hang in there and it will pass. You are always going to be their dad and they are always going to be your son or daughter. You are investing for the future.

MESSAGE FOR SOON-TO-BE DADS:
FATHERHOOD EQUALS FUN

There is an important group of dads we haven't directly addressed: future fathers. If you're a soon-to-be-dad who's reading this book in preparation for the birth of your first child, congratulations! You're in for a great ride.

For fathers-to-be, the advice is simple: Get lots of sleep (you're going to need it), and save your money (you're going to need lots of that, too). But whatever you do, don't spend too much time worrying about the fatherly obligations ahead. The costs of fatherhood are far outweighed by the rewards. And if you'd like proof, go find a highly involved dad and ask him if he relishes the big-shoulders job of being a responsible father. The answer you'll receive will give you all the assurance you need that fatherhood is, indeed, a blessing from above.

Being an involved dad is hard work (of course), but it's just about the most rewarding job any man can have.

"Ideas are the beginning points of all fortunes."

—

Napoleon Hill

CHAPTER 3

What Should We Talk About?

Setting the stage with topics that matter most.

Planning and thought should go into any worthwhile project we take on. The reality is we often just don't think when we begin something, or we simply act out of ignorance. I'm reminded of that reality when I read the following letter sent to an insurance company.

Dear Sirs,

I am writing in response to your request for additional information needed to complete my insurance claim. In block number 12 of the Medical Report Form, I just put "poor planning" as the cause of the accident. You said in your request for additional information that I should "explain more fully," and I trust that the following details will suffice.

I am a brick layer by trade. On the day of the accident, I was working alone on the roof of a new six-story building. When I completed my work, I discovered that I had about 500 pounds of brick left over. Rather than carry the bricks down six stories by hand, I decided to lower them in a barrel by using a pulley, which fortunately was attached to the side of the building at the sixth floor.

Securing the rope at the ground level, I went up to the roof, swung the barrel out and loaded the bricks into it. Then I went back to the ground and untied the rope, holding it tightly to insure a slow descent of the 500 pounds of brick. You will note in block number 11 of the accident report that I weigh 155 pounds.

Due to my surprise at being jerked off the ground so suddenly, I lost presence of mind and forgot to let go of the rope. Needless to say, I proceeded at a rapid rate up the side of the building.

In the vicinity of the third floor, I met the barrel coming down. This explains the fractured skull and broken collar bone.

Slowed only slightly, I continued my rapid ascent, not stopping until the fingers of my right hand were two knuckles deep in the pulley. Fortunately, by this time, I had regained my presence of mind and was able to hold tightly to the rope in spite of my pain. At approximately the same time, however, the barrel of bricks hit the ground and the bottom fell out of the barrel. Devoid of the weight of the bricks, the barrel now weighed approximately 50 pounds.

I refer again to my weight of 155 pounds as noted in block number 11. As you can imagine, I began a rapid descent down the side of the building. In the vicinity of the third floor, I met the barrel coming up. This accounts for the two fractured ankles and lacerations on my legs and lower body. The encounter with the barrel slowed me enough to lessen my injuries when I fell onto the pile of bricks, and fortunately, only three vertebrae were cracked.

I am sorry to report, however, that as I lay there on the bricks in pain, unable to stand, and watching the empty barrel six stories above me, I again lost my presence of mind, and let go of the rope.

Sincerely,

I.M. Sunk

Planning is important! Our kids are growing up **now** and we won't have a second chance to influence their young lives. With that in mind, we need to err on the side of being proactive. Sometimes we need to use the *Ready, Fire, Aim* approach.

The initial plan is merely to set aside the time to spend with them one-on-one. That is what I did. I didn't develop an overall plan for getting through all the material presented here. This list of topics just evolved out of our times together and the notes they took. We simply did Dad's Class one appointment at a time.

My situation may be dramatically different from yours. I knew that my children were getting excellent Bible teaching at school and church. I looked forward to building on that foundation with discussions about how to apply what they had already learned in real-life situations. I wanted them to learn how to integrate what they were learning into the greatest challenges of life— **dealing with money, people, their own self-image and faith.** The wisdom to do so can be found in the Scripture and personal experiences that you and others have had. It completes their education in very practical ways.

Over the past thirty years I have been blessed with the opportunity to travel, attending dozens of educational and ministry seminars and meet many interesting people. Some of those people have mentored Patty and me. One of my mentors, Bob Conklin, told me this truth many years ago: **Successful people figure out how things work, and then get on the 'good-side' of how things work.** I wanted my children to take what they were learning in church and school and apply it in the real world, in order to live a successful life of integrity—a life they could look back upon with pride.

The goal of Dad's Class is to impart wisdom through meaningful conversation. Some appointments with my sons and daughters were primarily recreational, others were structured around a specific concept I wanted them to grasp. The notes in their journals today reflect that as well. A single line on a page might mark a great afternoon; the next entry might be two full pages, a result of an hour-long visit over coffee.

Sometimes we discussed topics that the kids were dealing with at that particular time in their lives. At other times we were looking years into the future, talking about colleges and career choices, even when they were still in elementary school.

After looking back over the variety of topics discussed in our Dad's Class appointments and paging through the journals that our kids have kept, I have categorized the topics to give you some suggestions for talking to your sons and daughters. I've grouped the topics into these general headings that include the four major planes on which our lives function:

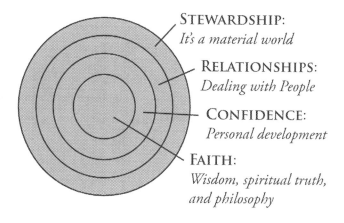

STEWARDSHIP:
It's a material world

RELATIONSHIPS:
Dealing with People

CONFIDENCE:
Personal development

FAITH:
Wisdom, spiritual truth, and philosophy

Who our children become largely depends upon **how they relate to other people, how they view the blessings in their lives, how they view themselves, and how they view God.** I am convinced that if they understood the impact of these subjects on their future, they would be asking the questions you will find in chapters four through seven of this book. You have the opportunity to initiate meaningful conversation about these important, character-defining concepts at every level.

In the next four chapters I have listed key ideas to serve as starters for your discussion times. These points obviously reflect my own particular beliefs and life philosophy. If they don't agree with your views, don't be afraid to address your perspective on the topic or delete the subject all together. Just because my personal views and yours do not necessarily match-up, does not mean the concept of Dad's Class won't have value for you and your kids.

I would begin by addressing the less personal and more universal **stewardship issues** with which we all have to deal in life. We can then move to the more important topics of building healthy relationships, self-image and personal confidence, and our relationship with and beliefs about God.

You'll note these four areas of our lives are deeply integrated. It's difficult to talk about money and our view of ownership without addressing how we view the world and the God who created it. How you relate to other people differs if you see people as some genetic accident, or individuals created in the image of God with an eternal destiny. As Jim Rohn says, *"Everything matters."* That is why we have so many things to talk about and why the list is so long. It could be much longer.

These topics, and the discussions they prompt, should be spiced with your own notes and stories that share your experiences. To help facilitate these discussions, I've marked each **talking point** or **key principle** with this symbol ❋ and left room for you to make your own notes in the margin of each of the pages that follow. I've also left plenty of room for you to add more topics that come to mind as you consider what's most important to you. I hope you find these suggestions helpful as you explore and build on them in your own personal way.

The topics you will find here are merely a collection of the entries that I have gleaned from the journals of my children. They should only be a starting point for you as you meet with your son or daughter. This is not a curriculum, but a list of topics and questions to serve as a resource to get you started. Remember that it is all about spending quality, concentrated, one-on-one time with them to make sure that they know how significant they are to you. You should remember as well that our children are always watching our every move, listening to every word and easily see through any hypocrisy in our lives.

I will never forget early one morning as a younger dad, when I was having a time of personal Bible study. Sarah, our first child, was less than 2 years old. I heard the pitter-patter of her bare feet running down the hallway carpet from her bedroom to see who was in the kitchen. I looked up in time to see her standing at the doorway rubbing her eyes, looking at me as if to say, "What are you doing?" Almost as soon as our eyes met, she turned around and ran back to her bedroom, where she retrieved her Gideon New Testament, and then came running back to the kitchen. Without a word spoken between us, she entered the kitchen, sat down in the middle of the floor, and began paging through her Bible. She couldn't read; she didn't really know what I was doing, but she was imitating my actions.

We all intuitively know the truth of the statement, "Modeling is the most effective method of teaching." Whether we intend to or not, our children are always watching us and our actions will always be more powerful than our words.

If you want your child to accept your values when he reaches his teen years, then you must be worthy of his respect during his younger years.
James Dobson

MORE ABOUT TALKING
TO YOUR CHILDREN

My number one responsibility is to evangelize my children.

James Dobson

Training is not telling, not teaching, not commanding, but something higher than all of these. It is not only telling a child what to do, but it is also showing him how to do it and seeing that it is done.

Andrew Murray

How you say it might be as important as what you say.

Harvey Mackay

We speak with more than our mouths. We listen with more than our ears.

Fred Rogers

Do you want to help your children reach the maximum potential that lies within them? Then raise them according to the precepts and values given to us in the Scriptures.

James Dobson

"If a person gets his attitude toward money straight,
it will help straighten out almost
every other area in his life."

Billy Graham

CHAPTER 4

Stewardship:
It's A Material World

*Financial Responsibility
and Dealing with the Reality
of How Things Work*

Money and the necessities, material possessions and comforts that it buys are realities with which we will deal throughout our lives. Understanding fundamental concepts of stewardship and responsible financial planning, at any age, is a huge advantage.

Zig Ziglar said, "Money isn't the most important thing in life, but it's reasonably close to oxygen on the 'gotta have it' scale." Actually, oxygen is a reasonable

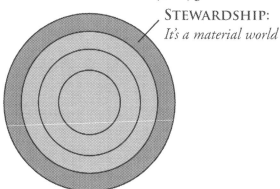

STEWARDSHIP:
It's a material world

comparison. What oxygen is to our physical bodies, money is to our economic survival. Acquiring increasing material assets throughout life becomes an obsession for some, far beyond their needs. Many in the world, however, merely survive from day to day because of extreme poverty. Where is the balance and what do we need to understand about our material world to be wise in dealing with it?

Dad's Notes

✳ **Begin with an understanding of who owns everything.**

Ownership is a term that implies the **sole authority over an asset.**

Stewardship is taking on **the responsibility of managing someone else's possessions.**

Concept: God owns it all, and we are the stewards of everything we have been given—not just money but other resources, our very lives, our health, our talents and abilities, our homes and our families.

Psalm 89:11: "The heavens are Yours, the earth also is Yours; The world and all it contains, You have founded them" (NASB).

As an act of good stewardship we choose to give back to God proportionately, as a testimony to Him that we recognize who the owner really is. *Note: The tithe is not mentioned in the New Testament except when Christ chastises the Pharisees for their legalistic use of the tithe on things as insignificant as "mint and dill and cumin."*

Great habits to cultivate are:

1. Giving the first ten percent to my church
2. Saving the second ten percent
3. Spending what's left over[1]

---

1) Patty and I had some interesting debates over giving our children total control over the 80 percent. She felt that they should have some controls put on how it was going to be spent. I wanted them to have the total freedom to make some mistakes <u>now</u> with the $8 they had from a $10 mowing job, rather than making those mistakes later on with thousands of dollars. I believe that "blowing" $8 on candy that makes you sick, and being left with empty pockets at the state fair can teach you a lesson that you will remember forever.

Dad's Notes

✳ **How do I handle money responsibly?**

Financial Show and Tell:

The invisible nature of money in today's economy is one of the major challenges in bringing young people to the point of understanding how finances work. My commission income comes in on a monthly basis as an **electronic transfer** into a checking account. My family and most of our children have never seen an electronic transfer and may not know how these work. On the other hand, we pay for the things **we buy with credit and debit cards, so many kids think that those cards represent an endless source of purchasing power.**

So what is the solution? Bring them to the point of understanding how finances work through Financial Show and Tell.

Show your checkbook or debit card statement to your son or daughter and **explain what they are and where the de-**

posits and withdrawals come from. Explain how they must balance to avoid going into the world of **insufficient funds.** Make sure they understand the fees that financial institutions charge for overdrafts and other services. Make it clear to them that:

Dad's Notes

If your outgo exceeds your income, your upkeep will become your downfall.

- Go over your credit card bills and show how costly a late payment can be, both in fees and interest charges, as well as in terms of the potential negative impact on your credit rating.
- Read through the fine print of the contract of a credit card offer and point out the traps that await the unknowing and unsuspecting.
- Tell stories of financial success through budgeting and thrift—like the story of Benjamin Franklin.

Dad's Notes

I like to tell her siblings the lesson our oldest daughter, Sarah, learned after receiving her first credit card bill, as it teaches a fundamental fact about the use of credit cards.

Just before leaving home as a college freshman, our daughter Sarah received her first credit card bill. As I recall, the total charges that she had made were less than $40. She knew that she needed to pay it off in full every month to avoid finance charges on the balance.

When I asked her about her payment, she indicated that she had it under control and that she'd "sent the payment in ON the due date." I knew immediately that we had a problem. Since it hadn't arrived at the credit card company prior to the due date, she was charged a $39 late payment fee.

I called the credit card company as soon as the late fee showed up on the next bill. They agreed to remove the late payment fee from the account, and Sarah learned a valuable lesson on the importance of paying your credit card billings in full, and in advance of the due date. That experience also encouraged me to help our children get a credit card of their own while still in high school. This gave us the opportunity to educate them about the challenges that await the naïve, how to use credit cards responsibly, and how to live within a budget.

Talk about:

- What is a checking account?[2]
- Why should I have one?
- How do you balance it?
- How do I use my ATM card?
- What is a PIN number?
- What's a money market, savings or investment account?
- How do credit cards work?[3]

2) *We made sure that our kids opened a checking account by the time they were 10 years old. I also wanted to make sure that they had a credit card during their high school years so that we had time to help them sort through what's involved in developing a credit rating, and how high interest rates and hidden fees prey on the ignorant.*

3) *After they get into college, they get inundated with credit card offers. The credit card companies know that if they default on their card, the parents of a minor are responsible for their debts. Don't become a victim of these questionable financial practices, but be proactive in educating your kids to the dangers of credit.*

Dad's Notes

✳ **Debt is a 4-Letter Word**

If you never borrow money, then you'll never be in debt.

Interest expense is what you pay to "rent" someone else's money.

Compound interest is either:

A) The *cost of interest on unpaid interest,* in which case it becomes a compounding debt if you are the borrower.

OR

B) The *interest on the interest you are paid* if you are a saver or investor who has invested in a savings or investment plan at a guaranteed rate of return.

Compound interest will work for savers and against borrowers. Based on the potential of compound interest, the best time to begin saving or investing is always the same—**NOW.**

The Rule of 72 is a simplified way to determine how long, at a fixed compound rate of interest, an investment or savings account will take to double its value.

This is arrived at by dividing 72 by the annual interest rate of return. For example: 72 divided by the assumed interest rate of eight percent, will estimate the invested amount will double in nine years.

$(72 \div 8 = 9)$

If you are purchasing a depreciating asset that does not generate income, then the interest expense is a total loss. If you use that asset as a necessary part of your business, which generates a profit, which more than offsets the interest expense, then you will be able to generate a net income through that investment.

Dad's Notes

❋ What are assets?

The value of your financial holdings is reflected in your **balance sheet** which shows assets (things of value) on the left and liabilities (debts you owe) on the right. The difference between the two is your **net worth** or **equity**.

Most of the things we own are depreciating assets:

- Cars
- Appliances
- Household furnishings
- Computers
- Clothing

Some assets normally appreciate:

- Real Estate
- Quality stocks and bonds (unless the market takes a huge loss as in 2008/2009)
- Well-managed business holdings

* **Begin with a plan on how you are going to spend your money.**

A budget is a plan that should include, at a minimum:
1. A tithe
2. Savings
3. Repayment of debts (if you have any)
4. Cost of living
5. Investments for the future

We will someday call the person who saves a portion of everything he earns **rich** and a person who spends all he earns **poor.** The power of saving a portion of all you earn is clearly seen in the book *The Richest Man in Babylon,* by George Samuel Clason. This book should be required reading for every young person. A more contemporary book that addresses this same concept is *The Automatic Millionaire* by David Bach.

Dad's Notes

※ **Profit is NOT a 4-Letter Word:**

I-E=P stands for
Income – Expenses = Profit

Income minus Expenses, equals Profit is the basic formula for any business enterprise.

Profit is the reward that comes to those who invest in business operations; it is a return on the investment and the risk that they take. All new business enterprises involve risk and rewards. These new businesses also generate jobs and those jobs, products, and services fuel the growth of our economy.

✳ **There are four great reasons to get a job:**

1. To earn immediate cash
2. To find out what you enjoy and don't enjoy doing
3. To learn new skills and increase your value in the marketplace
4. To build your resume and reputation

Note: We have never paid allowances, but always assured the kids that if they wanted to earn some money, there are always paying jobs to do. Whether it was babysitting next door, mowing lawns, working in our business office, stuffing mailings, detasseling corn, or working in food service, they've never lacked opportunities to work. I have always sought to creatively develop a "will to work" in our children, believing that a solid work ethic was one of the most important character traits that we could build into our kids. I am proud to say that each of them has an excellent reputation, based on what I have heard from the people for whom they have worked over the years.

Dad's Notes

A **Resume** is: a one or two page description of who you are, including highlights of your life and experiences to-date, as well as personal references.

- Your references can be teachers, coaches, administrators, bosses and friends.
- Your reputation is what you are known for.
- You are always building your reputation and your resume.

A paper boy in the U.S. is in the top one percent of the wealthy in the world because he has:

1. At least two meals today
2. A roof over his head
3. A regular source of income and
4. The opportunity for upward mobility

JOB: Just Over Broke

If you have a job and do not operate on a budget that allows you to pay your taxes, tithe, save, invest and **live on less than you earn in total,** you will be just over or actually someday, simply broke.

YOB: Your Own Business

Having a business of your own gives you an important advantage offered by our tax laws. In our nation, you are encouraged to invest in the future of your business as necessary to expand and create more jobs, commerce, and enterprise. For doing so, you are allowed to deduct those expenses before paying any taxes on the net income of your business each year.

The result of this is that many growing businesses, in their early years, can invest back into their growth virtually all potential profits, and pay very little or no income taxes.

This is a very different type of taxation than that experienced by a person who is an employee and paid a salary or commission income by an employer. The employed person pays income tax on the first dollar he earns, and it is usually with-

Dad's Notes

held from his very first paycheck. He has deductions that are basically limited to:

- mortgage interest deductions on his primary residence
- charitable contributions

✳ **Diversify your investments.**

Solomon's advice was to divide your wealth into seven or eight parts, so that you would not have all of your assets in one basket. This is good advice for any investor today. Diversification of investments will help you manage the risks of ownership.

Eccl. 11:2-3 says "Divide your portion to seven, or even to eight, for you do not know what misfortune may occur on the earth" (NASB).

✳ The First Law of Economics: "There ain't no free lunch."

Whether you are talking about an individual or a society, you cannot get something for nothing. Even if something appears to be free, there is always a cost to the person or to society as a whole—even though that cost may be hidden.

✳ What is insurance[4] and how does it work?

Why do we need to have:
* Health insurance?
* Life insurance?
* Car insurance?
* Liability insurance?

What is a **premium**?
What is a **deductible**?

---

4) *A basic understanding of insurance is necessary and most kids do not grasp a practical understanding until they get into college and are offered the opportunity to take a business course entitled, "**Risk Management 101**." By then, they should have life insurance, health insurance and car insurance in force. If they aren't already covered with these policies, the young adults need to recognize that insurance will become a major expense in their future. The sooner they get an understanding of the basics, the better.*

Dad's Notes   ✳ **Taxes**

This is how we fund our government, in order to provide military protection and services that can most effectively provide for our citizens—like roads, schools, police and fire protection, clean water and sewer services. We typically pay taxes when we buy:

- Gasoline, tobacco products, and luxury items
- Phone and other services
- Any item to which the state attaches a sales tax
- Property that we own, including real estate

In addition, we pay taxes to the city, state, and federal government.

The Tax Foundation monitors the timing of "Tax Freedom Day" each year. In 2009 Tax Freedom Day fell on April 13th. That means Americans worked three months and 13 days, from January 1 to April 13 during 2009 (or 28% of the year) to earn enough money to pay that year's tax obligations at the federal, state and local levels. Americans will pay more in taxes than they will spend on food, clothing, and housing combined.[5]

✳ Political Parties & Our Democracy

The levels of government:
- City
- County
- State
- National

The Branches of our Federal Government:
- Executive: our President
- Legislative: our Congress
- Judicial: our Court System

5) *www.taxfoundation.org*

Dad's Notes

Democrats are sometimes called liberal, progressive, and are more apt to expect and support government involvement in social action, and promote financial support for those programs through tax dollars.

Republicans are called conservative, and seek to minimize taxes, believing that private charities and local communities can sufficiently address social issues.

How do you become involved in the political party of your choice?

- County delegate registration
- County Convention
- State Convention
- National Convention
- Committees at each level

Q: Why should you get involved in the political process?

A: Participation and voting in *every* primary and general election is a responsibility, not just a right we enjoy.

A: The person who has the right to vote and doesn't is no better off than the person who is denied that right.

A: It is the duty of every citizen to become fully engaged in the process.

A: Those who do not become involved in the process *"lose all griping rights!"*

❊ Cars

Second only to their home, the purchase of an automobile is the largest single expenditure that most people make in their lifetime. You should know the basics of how your car runs and what it takes to care for your vehicle if you are blessed to have one.

The systems on your automobile:

- **Fuel System:** fill up the tank regularly or walk—and use the right fuel.

Dad's Notes

- **Cooling System:** where the radiator is, what it does and how to keep from getting burned, by never attempting to open a hot one.

- **Lubrication System:** why checking the oil may be necessary, how to do it, and what to do if you are low.

- **Air Intake System:** the location of the air cleaner and what happens if your car cannot "breathe" correctly.

- **Braking System:** how to bring things to a halt.

- **Electrical System:** how the battery, spark plugs and lights work together to get us from here to there.

- **Tires:** proper inflation is important. Check 'em.

- **Speedometer:** always make sure it is well below the legal limit.

- **Seat belts & air bags:** they are there when you need them— which is always!

Note: These are a couple of field trip topics, especially for those girls and guys that are getting close to driving age. It gives them an appreciation for what goes into buying a car and how to keep it running. The need for a friendly, trustworthy mechanic should become obvious. Introduce them to yours.

Owning a car has additional associated costs:

- Sales taxes
- Registration, tax and fees
- License plates
- Insurance
- Maintenance
- Fuel

Note: Discuss how much each of these can cost and what affects them. Even a "junker," that someone might give you for free, has a high cost of ownership. What affects the insurance? Why do some teens pay $200-$400 per month just for insurance premiums? Take a tour of a used car lot and a new car showroom as a backdrop to your Dad's Class outing and discuss these topics as you "consider the cost." As a real-life example of these costs, pull the purchase agreement, registration, service receipts and insurance policy out for your family vehicles and go over each of these items with your son or daughter.

Dad's Notes

✳ **Buying a home**

This is the single largest investment that most people ever make.

Why should I consider buying a home?

What are the steps in buying a home?

- Accumulating a down payment of at least 10-20 percent by living on less than you earn and saving the rest.
- Weigh the advantages of a realtor and select one who is experienced and trustworthy.
- Shop the market to determine what you can afford in your area.
- Locate a reputable, qualified mortgage lender in order to determine if you can obtain the financing you will need. Find out at this time the interest rate that you will qualify for and any "points" or added costs that they might assess on your loan at origination. There are sometimes hidden fees so read the fine print.

- Select a property that meets your needs, some of your wants, and is a good value.
- Make the offer, usually below the asking price. Make counter offers if necessary, or be willing to shop additional homes.
- When you come to an agreement with a seller, close the purchase.
- Work with your realtor and lender to complete the necessary closing, insurance, property tax, and escrow accounts.
- Recognize that there will be moving expenses and perhaps the necessary purchase of furniture, drapes, and appliances that are a part of buying your home.
- Mortgage payments must be paid on a monthly basis on time to assure that you maintain an excellent credit rating. It's your financial reputation and it's hard to build up and easy to lose with slow or missed payments.

Dad's Notes

Dad's Notes

- Refinancing is sometimes advisable when interest rates drop or your lending institution has a program for doing so at a reasonable cost.

- Equity is the value of a piece of property over and above any mortgage or other liabilities relating to it. The amount of your equity in a property will grow as your mortgage shrinks over time and the value of the property appreciates.

Both of our sons must have picked up on the value of "appreciating assets" and especially real estate as a sound, long term investment. Both Adam and Jordan purchased their first homes before their 19th birthdays and had to wait to close on their homes until they turned 19, as that is the age of majority in our state. Adam's was a 3-bedroom home just three miles from us. He lived there with two to three other guys until he and his wife took over the house. Jordan saw the opportunity to become a landlord and purchased an older home that was turned into a four-unit apartment house. He lived in one unit and rented out the other three, which covered his mortgage payment. His interest in real estate led to his first full-time job as a leasing agent for a local company. He has also worked as a property manager and earned his real estate license. Prior to his marriage in 2008 Jordan purchased a second home that had been converted into a duplex.

✳ **Is stewardship limited to money and the "stuff" that we accumulate?**

NO! The principles of good stewardship apply to every blessing with which our life has been blessed. How can we apply them to:

- Our physical body and health?
- Our mind, the education and skills we have acquired?
- Our special talents and abilities that come so naturally to us?
- Our personality?
- The family, community, state and nation in which we live?

MORE ABOUT STEWARDSHIP

A steward is one who manages another's resources. Each of us is a manager, not an owner. God is the owner, and we are to manage according to His plan.

Larry Burkett

Success has nothing to do with what you gain in life or accomplish for yourself. It's what you do for others.

Danny Thomas

If our charities do not at all pinch or hamper us, I should say they are too small. There ought to be things we should like to do and cannot do because our charitable expenditure excludes them.

C. S. Lewis

God will withdraw resources from the poor stewards, as related in Matthew 25, and give it to the good stewards.

Bill Bright

Christians have become victims of one of the most devious plots Satan ever created—the concept that money belongs to us and not to God.

Larry Burkett

"You can get everything in life that you want,
if you will just help enough other people
get what they want."

―――

Bob Conklin

CHAPTER 5

Relationships:
Dealing with People

Developing People Skills & Healthy Relationships

So much of our life is spent in relationship with others that developing the skills necessary to build and sustain positive, productive relationships is vital to a successful life. We think instinctively about the impact that these skills have in the work place, but they are even more critical within your family, your school, church, and personal relationships. Two great commands in the Bible address the two most profound relationships we all experience:

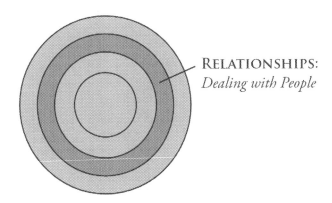

RELATIONSHIPS:
Dealing with People

"Love God and love your neighbor as yourself." Learning how to obey those commands should be life-long goals for each of us. Share what you've learned with your kids. Not just your successes, but your failures as well. They need to know that you are human and you have survived some disasters. It will give them the confidence that they can too.

- What have been your greatest relational failures?
- What have been the most successful relationships you have had during your lifetime to date?
- What have you learned from these that you can share?

For additional space to answer these questions and write your story turn to the My Story section the back of the book.

✳ Remember the best source of experience is OPE (Other People's Experience).

Why? Because the cost of personal experience is often too high. Watching cause and effect working in the lives of others can be a great teacher and a short-cut to living a more successful and satisfying life.

The Bible is filled with stories of people who lived wisely and those who lived foolishly, as well as those whose lives were a mixture of both. How would the life of David have been different if he had not fallen into lust, adultery and murder? How would it have affected his life and the kingdom of Israel? The biographies of great men and women of today can give you the wisdom of OPE as well.

✳ **Effective Communication is the key to human relationships.**

Communication is your key to success in the information age in which we live. Whether you are attempting to communicate in conversation (even in Dad's Class), via e-mail, instant messaging, Facebook, text message, in a meeting or conference setting, you have to be able to create an opportunity for a "meeting of the minds."

The format is always the same and it includes at least five steps:

1. **Identify** with your audience.
2. **Tell the story** of your product, plan, program or service.
3. **Share** a testimony of **how** you, or someone you know, had a problem that was solved by your product, plan, program or service.
4. **Why** this is important to you (or someone whose story you are sharing) and to your audience.

5. **Ask** them to make a **decision**. It
might just be a decision to listen
more or get more information.

Tell

Identify → Your Story → How? → Why? → *Decision*

✳ **The principle of reciprocity**

Generosity in life is not just the right
thing to do and the nice thing to do, but
it turns out, it's the smart way to live.
Check out these teachings of the sages
that indicate what goes out of your life
will return **in kind**:

"You can get everything in life that you
want, if you will just help enough other
people get what they want."

Bob Conklin (from his book
How to Get People to Do Things)

Dad's Notes

"People don't care how much you know, until they know how much you care."

Cavett Roberts

The point is the same. If you want to lead, serve others. To the degree that you meet the needs of others, you will be blessed. Scripture says it best, in the words of Christ Himself:

"Give, and it will be given to you. They will pour into your lap a good measure—pressed down, shaken together, and running over. For by your standard of measure it will be measured to you in return."

Luke 6:38 (NASB)

"Cast your bread on the surface of the waters, for you will find it after many days."

Eccl. 11:1 (NASB)

❋ **People don't respond positively to criticism.** Be careful to choose your words wisely and well. Scripture refers to words as "arrows" for good reason. Like arrows, once launched their damage is done and they cannot be retrieved. Many friends and families have been divided by harsh words spoken in the heat of the moment.

"Let no unwholesome word proceed from your mouth, but only such a word as is good for edification according to the need of the moment, so that it will give grace to those who hear. Do not grieve the Holy Spirit of God, by whom you were sealed for the day of redemption. Let all bitterness and wrath and anger and clamor and slander be put away from you, along with all malice. Be kind to one another, tender-hearted, forgiving each other, just as God in Christ also has forgiven you."
Eph. 4:29-32 (NASB)

A European scholar, Johann Paul Freidrich, wrote two centuries ago: "If a

Dad's Notes

child tells a lie, tell him he has told a lie, but don't call him a liar. If you define him as a liar, you break down his confidence in his own character." By restricting criticism to a specific bad act, a parent is unlikely to damage a child's self image.

This is not only true with children, it is true of people in general. They typically *strive to live up to your expectations of them* and if you distinguish between something they did and who they are, it makes an important difference in how they view you.

"Criticize things, not people."

Zig Ziglar

- Critics aren't leaders.

- There's never been a statue erected to a critic.

- There is no such thing as "constructive criticism."

A better bet is to praise people and keep a positive focus:

"Finally, brethren, whatever is true, whatever is honorable, whatever is right, whatever is pure, whatever is lovely, whatever is of good repute, if there is any excellence and if anything worthy of praise, dwell on these things."
Phil. 4:8 (NASB)

✳ How to win friends

"Two things will influence your life. The people you meet and the books you read."

Charlie "Tremendous" Jones

You become like the people with whom you surround yourself, so choose your friends wisely. They will have a powerful impact on your life.

Dad's Notes   A great book was published by Dale Carnegie in 1936 entitled, *How to Win Friends and Influence People.* It's still a best seller today, and one that I recommend often. It is a core part of the Dale Carnegie Course still being taught today.[6]

Six ways to make people like you:

(from *How To Win Friends and Influence People*)

1. Become genuinely interested in other people.
2. Smile.
3. Remember that a man's name is to him the sweetest and most important sound in any language.
4. Be a good listener. Encourage others to talk about themselves.
5. Talk in the terms of the other man's interest.
6. Make the other person feel important and do it sincerely.

6) *In our home we encourage the kids to read by paying them for specific books.* How to Win Friends and Influence People *is high on my list of books that I recommend, and I give a copy of this book to each of the kids for their future reference.*

✳ Be a leader.

- Never point out a problem or complain about something, unless you have a suggestion for solving it.

- Don't be a part of the problem, be a part of the solution.

✳ "The one who asks the best questions, wins."

Bobb Biehl

Communication is a key to successful relationships. I've come to believe that the key in communication is to **become a great listener.** In sales, where I have lived for almost thirty-five years, I've learned this truth:

The answer to most questions is really five or six questions deep. The question is usually, *"Why?"*

Dad's Notes

✳ **When you ask an intelligent question, it communicates:**

- Interest
- Attention
- A willingness to learn
- Humility

A person to whom you have asked a reasonable and thoughtful question, will be forced to engage in thought. Even if they choose not to answer the question, they cannot refuse to think about the answer. That's why questions are so powerful in communication.

✳ **The R-Factor Question**

(developed by Dan Sullivan of The Strategic Coach™) is the most powerful question I have ever encountered. This is the question:

"If we were sitting here three years from today, what would need to have happened in your life, personally and professionally, for you to feel happy with your success?"

The power of the R-factor question is its ability to generate a powerful process of thinking and an answer that casts vision.

- People will begin to envision what needs to happen in their lives for them to feel happy three years from today. Only they can define happiness for them, so their answer will be unique to them.

- That process forces them to cast vision for themselves, generating positive emotions in the present from the hope that these thoughts produce.

- They then have the choice to share their hopes and goals with you. If they choose to do so, it's an indication that your *R*elationship (that's why it's called the *R*-factor

Dad's Notes

question) with them is good and growing, and it gives you the opportunity to build on that relationship as you help them to reach their goals over the next three years.

✳ Everyone has a warped perspective.

"Perception is more important than reality."

Henry Kissinger

Perception is important, because people tend to act on their perception. That is why it is more important than reality. If someone pulled the fire alarm, we would run out of the building, because there is a perception of danger.

Perception is as individual as our fingerprints. That's why effective communication is so challenging and difficult. It is also why effective communicators tend to become leaders and people who are paid well for their ability to influence others.

"All miscommunication is the result of differing assumptions."

Dr. Jerry Ballard

Whenever there is a void of information, there is always conjecture; and the conjecture is always negative. Another way of expressing that thought is:

Ignorance breeds suspicion.

Because this tendency is our nature, always attempt to follow the advice of Steve Covey in his book *Seven Habits of Highly Effective People.* Habit number five is: "Seek first to understand (i.e. listen) and then to be understood." This is the path to getting "on the same page" with others.

Dad's Notes

✳ **The relationship decisions you make will chart the course for your life.**

My friend Bill Sapp has told me that the person you choose to marry is the second most important decision you will make in this lifetime. The first and most important decision is what you will do with the invitation to put your faith and trust in Jesus Christ for your eternal destiny. That decision will determine, according to Scripture, whether you will spend eternity in heaven or hell. In a similar way, the second decision, who you marry, will determine whether *this life* will be like heaven or hell on earth!

The quality of your major life decisions will be based largely on your ability to judge the character of the people with whom you associate. Choose your friends, business associates, and spouse with care.

MORE ABOUT FRIENDSHIPS

In order to have friends, you must first be one.

Elbert Hubbard

I have found that the closer I am to the godly people around me, the easier it is for me to live a righteous life because they hold me accountable.

John MacArthur

Yes, the Spirit was sent to be our Counselor. Yes, Jesus speaks to us personally. But often he works through another human being.

John Eldredge

We shall never have friends if we expect to find them without fault.

Thomas Fuller

In each of my friends there is something that only some other friend can fully bring out. By myself I am not large enough to call the whole man into activity; I want other lights than my own to show all his facets.

C. S. Lewis

More About Making Wise Decisions

Life is built on character, but character is built on decisions.

Warren Wiersbe

Successful people make right decisions early and manage those decisions daily.

John Maxwell

When confronted with a decision, write down the pros and cons, cancel them out one against the other, then take the course indicated by what remains.

Ben Franklin

It is the nature, and the advantage, of strong people that they can bring out the crucial questions and form a clear opinion about them. The weak always have to decide between alternatives that are not their own.

Dietrich Bonhoeffer

It is always your next move.

Napoleon Hill

"Inaction breeds doubt and fear.
Action breeds confidence and courage."

———

Dale Carnegie

CHAPTER 6

Confidence:
Personal Development

The Key to Growth and Personal Development

All development is self-development. It is based on the foundational belief that you are personally responsible for investing the life, talents, and abilities with which God has blessed you, to make the most of your life—not just for your own benefit, but for the greater good. Next to knowing who you are *in Christ*, the most important thing you need to know is *yourself.* What are your strengths and abilities? Character qualities? How you can cultivate habits that help you make the most of those personal assets is what personal development is all about.

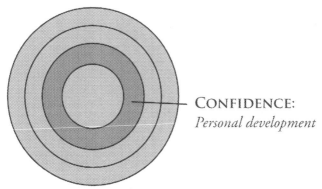

CONFIDENCE:
Personal development

John Goddard

Nothing inspires personal confidence more than setting and achieving personal goals over a lifetime. **Life really is *a confidence game.* Those who succeed are those who have the confidence to believe they can succeed and the vision to cast a future that keeps their interest until their goals are reached.** John Goddard's story has inspired me since I first heard it over 25 years ago.

One rainy afternoon an inspired 15-year old boy named John Goddard[7] sat down at his kitchen table in Los Angeles and wrote three words at the top of a yellow pad, **"My Life List."** Under that heading he wrote down 127 goals that he wanted to achieve in his lifetime. Among them:

- climb Mt. Everest;
- explore the Nile;
- study primitive tribes in the Sudan;
- explore the Great Barrier Reef of Australia;
- climb Cheop's Pyramid;
- circumnavigate the globe;
- run a five-minute mile;

7) *Learn more about John's progress at: www.johngoddard.info and read about his adventures in his book,* The survivor: 24 Spine-Chilling adventures on the Edge of Death ©2001.

- dive in a submarine;
- read the Bible from cover to cover;
- play 'Clair de Lune' on the piano;
- write a book;
- read the entire 'Encyclopedia Britannica' from cover to cover.

Idle dreaming? Not to Goddard. Goddard became one of the greatest explorers and adventurers in the world.

- He was the first man to explore the entire length of the Nile and Congo Rivers.
- He climbed the Matterhorn in a blizzard that was so bad, not even the professional climbers would go along.
- He retraced the route of Marco Polo through all of the Middle East, Asia and China.
- He has lived with 260 different tribal groups, ranging from the headhunters of New Guinea to the pygmies of Central Africa to the hippies of Tempe.
- At last count, John Goddard had accomplished 114 of his original 127 goals.

Just as important in John's story is to understand that he has never stopped setting new goals. Today his list has grown to over 600 goals, of which he has accomplished over 500. During 2008 John reached goals number 550 and 551 by visiting Petra in Jordan and standing in the Jordan river where Jesus was baptized by John the Baptist.

Pursuing his goals hasn't been without danger. Goddard has been bitten by a rattlesnake, charged by an elephant, and trapped in quicksand. He has crashed in planes, been caught in earthquakes, and almost drowned twice while running rapids. But his overwhelming desire to discover fresh knowledge and to complete his youthful list of goals drives him on in spite of the danger.

Still to go: visit every country of the world (he has 30 left), climb Mt. Everest, explore the entire lengths of the Yangtse River in China, the Niger in Africa and the Orinoco in Venezuela, visit the North and South Poles, and visit the moon.

My wife Patty and I had, what we consider one of the highlights of a lifetime when we were invited into John Goddard's home and given a tour of the memorabilia that he has collected during his adventures. Afterwards we went with him on a four-mile hike near his home in Los Angeles. John and his wife Carol were gracious hosts; and he demonstrates the confident humility that comes from having achieved over 500 specific goals in his life, **to date.** In my conversations with John, he never says, "Good-bye" but always leaves you with: "*To be continued.*"

✳ **There is no more empowering school in which to enroll, than in the *School of Your Own Goals.***
Because whenever you set and achieve a goal of your own, you engage in the process of becoming a different person. You learn new skills, gain determination, and increase your confidence with each goal accomplished.

Dad's Notes

✳ **The goals we set determine the direction in which our lives move.**

"Man is a goal-seeking animal…and his life only has meaning as he is striving and reaching out to achieve his goals…"
Aristotle

Goals should be set in six key areas of our life:

1. Spiritual
2. Physical
3. Mental
4. Social
5. Family
6. Financial

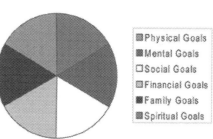

A Balanced Life

☐ Physical Goals
■ Mental Goals
☐ Social Goals
☐ Financial Goals
■ Family Goals
■ Spiritual Goals

Dad's Notes

Goals are: Objectives or desires that you set before you—your desires.

Success is: The progressive realization of worthwhile goals.

A "Goal Line": A series of progressive short and long term goals that you have set for yourself. They will take you from where you are today to where you want to be in one, three, five, ten, twenty-five years or a lifetime, with God's blessing.

These goals are progressive and enable you to learn new skills, develop latent talents, and discover new abilities that will make you a person who is able to set larger and more significant goals in the future.

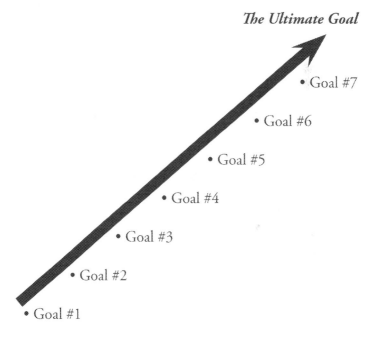

The Ultimate Goal

• Goal #7

• Goal #6

• Goal #5

• Goal #4

• Goal #3

• Goal #2

• Goal #1

Dad's Notes

A "Goal Line" helps me to recognize that every worthwhile goal that I have should ideally be positioning me to go on to achieve my next goal.

Dad's Notes

※ **Steps in setting goals:**

1. **Brainstorm** by making a list of at least 100 things that you want to do, places you want to go, people you want to meet. Think in terms of the six areas listed previously. Don't think too small. Remember John Goddard's "Life List" he created at 15 and think big!

2. **Sort, categorize, prioritize and evaluate** this list over several days.

3. **Set one, three, five or ten-year goals** that you would like to commit yourself to achieving.

4. **Develop a plan, visualize the accomplishment of these goals, and go to work** on them to systematically achieve your goals, one at a time.

5. **Review your goals and evaluate your progress** periodically, altering your goals, plans or methods as needed to achieve them.

The **Life Extender**™ by Dan Sullivan of the Strategic Coach™, says that the three things that affect when people die are:

- Lack of goals
- Lack of friends
- Lack of money or a plan

If you don't have a plan for your life—other people will.

If you don't know where you're going, any road will get you there.

Your subconscious mind is programmed by consciously focusing your mind on inspiring, God-honoring goals that you can visualize. Jesus said,

"It shall be done to you according to your faith."

Matt 9:29 (NASB)

Dad's Notes

"If one advances confidently in the direction of his dreams, and endeavors to live the life which he has imagined, he will meet with a success unexpected in common hours."

Henry David Thoreau

✳ Discover your unique ability.

Foundational to Dan Sullivan's Strategic Coach program is the idea of your "unique ability." Dan would tell you that there are certain things that you are *"just not very good at..."* but that's OK, because we all have things we aren't very good at doing. There are things that each of us does that we would be considered competent at. However, there are others who can perform those tasks just as well as we can. But there are things that you are able to do with "excellence or even genius" quality. It is because of your ability in those areas that people want to develop a relationship with you, hire you, or do business with you. An important objective in

your life should be to discover what it is
that you naturally do exceptionally well.
Find out how to utilize that talent in your
life and do it over and over and over.

Dad's Notes

To discover your unique ability:

- Think about those tasks you do
  that you enjoy. Even though they
  are difficult for some, you find
  you don't get tired, but rather
  gain energy from doing them.

- Ask others what they think you
  are good at, and what they ad-
  mire about you.

- Take a career test or two and
  discover what these psychological tests reveal to you concerning
  your talents and aptitudes.

- Look for classes, jobs or hobbies
  that give you a chance to develop
  what appear to be your unique
  abilities.

✳ **Determine what motivates you, and pursue it.**

In the book *Rich Dad, Poor Dad,* author Robert T. Kiyosaki talks about how people work for either:

- security,
- comfort, or
- wealth.

Those that want security will look for a good job with good benefits, and hopefully a secure 401K or other retirement program. They want to avoid any risk and as a result, they will avoid most great opportunities that might come across their path.

Those that want a few more comforts—like the better than average income, a second home, a few vacations every year and better things for their families, will have to take a few risks. Like the book by Stanley and Danko, *The Millionaire Next Door* reveals, they'll probably end up starting their own business and

taking advantage of leverage and the tax
advantages offered to business owners.

But if you want to be a part of the
third group—the wealthy—you'll need
to take a few risks, make security a sec-
ondary priority, and set and achieve larger
goals than the average person.

Dad's Notes

In his book *Cashflow Quadrant,*
Kiyosaki outlines the four groups of
people that exist, who have very different
views of work, income, money and their
personal economy.

The first is the employed person, who
trades their time and skills for money
on a regular basis. Whether they are
an emergency room doctor, a dentist,
an attorney, an accountant, a carpen-
ter or a custodian, they all perform
their duties, submit a bill to their employer or client, and then do it again.
If they ever stop working, their income stops.

Dad's Notes

The second type of person is the self-employed. While this person has the tax advantages that come with being a business owner, they are still in the process of trading their time and talents for a paycheck. If they are fortunate enough to be able to develop some equity in a business that they can sell upon their retirement, they may capture some retained earnings or savings as well.

The third type of person is the big business owner, who has a business that they could leave for a year or more; and the business would continue to provide them with an income in their absence, and even continue to grow.

The fourth type of person is the investor. This is the person who takes his wealth and continues to reinvest in business ventures, real-estate, stocks, and other growth assets that will provide portfolio income and equity growth on an on-going basis.

✳ **Three ways to process our thoughts and gain perspective and direction:**

1. Write things down (journaling)
2. Talk things out (counsel with godly friends)
3. Pray (talk things out with God)

✳ **Your self-image is important**
because we all intuitively seek to live up to our own self-image. You will act like the person you believe you are!

✳ **Know thyself:**
This phrase has been attributed to several Greek scholars, and it means that we are to pursue an understanding of our basic temperament, gifts, talents, strengths, etc.

Dad's Notes

Are you Sanguine, Choleric, Phlegmatic or Melancholy?

These are labels used to describe the four basic temperaments:

Sanguine: outgoing personality that likes attention.

Choleric: goal oriented, driven personality.

Phlegmatic: Laid back, calm, easy going.

Melancholy: Sensitive, artistic, feeling personality.

We are all a combination of at least two or more of these in varying proportions that make each of our personalities unique.

(For more information read Spirit Controlled Temperament *by Tim LaHaye.)*

What are your strongest tendencies, abilities, motivators, and values?

What's my learning style? Do I respond best to:

Visual: I learn best by watching.
Auditory: I prefer to learn by listening.
Kinesthetic: I want to learn by "hands-on" experience.

✳ Who am I?

I am the sum of:

- The natural gifts and abilities I possess.
- The purpose and goals that I have set for myself.
- The skills and abilities I have mastered.
- The successes I have achieved.
- The reputation I have developed.

Dad's Notes

※ **How do others define who I am?**

Intelligence is the "smarts" God has given you, which is interpreted by educators as an I.Q. or score on an ACT or SAT. However, that is not who you are. You are much more than a score on any test!

Gifts are those natural abilities to do certain things well. They are God-given.

Skills are abilities that you have learned. They include:

1. How to use the computer.
2. How to write effectively.
3. How to speak before a group.
4. How to wash clothes, clean house and cook.
5. How to babysit, mow the yard, or paint your room.

✳ Suggestions to live by:

1. Have an eternal perspective
2. Question your own motivation
3. Do the right thing
4. Simplify your life
5. Have a sense of humor

Ask yourself in each case "why?"

Dad's Notes

✳ Urgent/Not Urgent
Important/Not Important

There's a diagram in Steven Covey's, *7 Habits of Highly Effective People* that really helps bring home the importance of using wisdom in determining how you are going to spend your time and your life. All tasks are *not* equally important.

Planning wisely means that we invest time in those things that are not urgent, but which are important and require us to plan ahead and "live life on purpose."

Not Urgent & Not Important	Not Urgent & Important
Urgent & Not Important	Urgent & Important

Determine what things in your life would fall into each of these four categories. Then determine which are using most of your time. Are there changes you would like to make in how you spend your time? What would the impact be if you did?

"There are times that you will not be able to explain to anyone what God is leading you to do."

Howard Hendricks

"Whether it's the best of times or the worst of times, it's the only time we've got."

Art Buchwald

Dad's Notes ✳ **Ignorance or stupidity?**

Have you ever caught yourself thinking someone is just plain stupid? Are they really, or are they just ignorant?

Stupid—refers to a person of extremely low IQ. While there are people that qualify by that definition, most people who are labeled in that way are not stupid.

Ignorant—refers to a person's lack of knowledge on a particular subject. If you take the time to think before calling someone stupid, you will most likely realize that they are just ignorant.

So what can be done to remedy that situation?

Perhaps the responsibility to enlighten them is yours.

✳ **Two-step formula for success:**

1. Pray like it all depends on God.
2. Work like it all depends on you.

✳ **Your reputation is all you will have at the end of your life.**
And when you look back, I believe that it will all rest on your mastery of:

Dan Sullivan's
Four "Referability Traits"
Dan Sullivan, who mentors entrepreneurs in his Strategic Coach™ Program, refers often to the Four Referability Traits that we all need to develop if we're going to be successful in life:

1. Show up...on-time!

Showing up may sound elementary, but many people don't!

Dad's Notes

2. Do what you say you're going to do!

Be a person of your word and of integrity. If you say you are going to do something, the people who know you by reputation should know that what you have promised to do is as good as done.

3. Follow every transaction through to completion!

This is where most people fail. They quit too soon. They don't persevere.

"Nothing in this world can take the place of persistence. Talent will not; nothing is more common than unsuccessful people with talent. Genius will not; unrewarded genius is almost a proverb. Education will not; the world is full of educated derelicts. Persistence and determination alone are omnipotent. The slogan 'press on' has solved and always will solve the problems of the human race."

President Calvin Coolidge

4. Say "Please" and "Thank You."   **Dad's Notes**

Sounds simple doesn't it? Ever noticed how uncommon it is that people you deal with say "thank you"? Don't you think more favorably and highly of those who do? Jesus himself experienced this, as recorded in Luke 17:11-19. After healing ten lepers, only one took time to return, praise God and thank Christ for this miracle—and he was a Samaritan, one who was despised by the Jews.

These four referability traits are so called because if you live your life, or lead your business by these commitments, people will not only want to be associated with you, causing you to prosper and be highly respected, but they will recommend you to others as well.

Dad's Notes

✳ **Your reputation**

It is all you have on which to base your good name.

Life is a do-it-yourself project.

"It takes many good deeds to build a good reputation, and only one bad one to lose it."

Benjamin Franklin

A good reputation takes a lifetime to develop and can be destroyed in an instant.

You will have sufficient challenges in your life with which to deal without creating your own, through one bad decision—or a series of bad decisions.

There is a proverb that is worth contemplating:

Plant a thought, reap an action,
Plant an action, reap a habit,
Plant a habit, reap a character,
Plant a character, reap a destiny.

What would you like your reputation to reflect?

How would you like others to describe you at your funeral?

- Faithful?
- Unselfish?
- Outgoing?
- Friendly?
- Honest?
- Self-controlled?
- Reliable?
- Clean?
- Joyful?

✳ **How to determine God's purpose for your life.**

1. Identify our purpose in life as defined by Scripture:
- Glorify God (1 Cor. 6:20)
- Love the Lord (1 Cor. 2:9)
- Be "salt and light" (Matt. 5:13-14)

Dad's Notes

2. Ask and search for your specific purpose:
- Fast and pray.
- Look for how God might use you to advance His kingdom and purposes.
- Look for ways to help other believers.
- Look for ways to be faithful in little ways.
- Look for ways to serve others.
- Look for confirmation by witnesses.
- Look for clarity over time.
- Your direction may go through the "death of a vision."
- It may mean dying to your own desires (John 12:24).
- It will be related to your spiritual gift.

✳ Sympathy vs. Empathy

Sympathy is feeling sorry or sad for or with someone.

Empathy is when you understand someone else's problem without feeling the way they do about it.

Understanding the difference and cultivating your ability to empathize with someone is a powerful skill. Why?

✳ Positive focus
A great way to start any conversation is to ask for positive feedback.

- What's the most exciting thing going on in your life right now?
- What are you looking forward to?
- What are you most thankful for right now?

Dad's Notes

✳ **Successful people**

"…are ordinary people with an extraordinary amount of determination."

Dr. Robert Schuller

✳ **Habits not discipline**

Our life is the result of our habits—positive or negative. That is why creating positive habits is so important.

"Successful people are those people who are willing to do the unpleasant things that unsuccessful people won't do, and those unpleasant things only become less unpleasant to the degree that they become a habit."

Bob Conklin

"We are all perfectly disciplined to our current set of habits."

Dan Sullivan

"People are about as happy as they make up their minds to be."

Abe Lincoln

"Everything matters."

Jim Rohn

"When you are green, you grow; when you are ripe you rot."

Ray Kroc

※ **Always be prepared:**

Ziggy says, "It's always better to have it and not need it, than to need it and not have it." (i.e., be prepared—maybe even over prepared).

"The plan is nothing; the planning is everything. No battle plan survives contact with the enemy."
A 19th Century Prussian General von Moltke often quoted by both Eisenhower and Churchill during WWII

※ **MFA—Motivation Follows Action**
Some of us need to take action and then the motivation will follow.

Dad's Notes

✳ **Your perceived "success" in life is the accumulative result of:**

- The gifts God gave you at birth, your unique:
  - » Mind
  - » Body
  - » Spirit
  - » Family
  - » Genetic traits

- The friends you make.
- The education you receive.
- The decisions you make (college, career, spouse, family, etc.).
- The wisdom you have gained and thoughtfully acted on.
- The ways in which you have dealt with the challenges of life, endured and learned from them. Remember that it "rains on the just and the unjust."
- The work in which you have invested.
- The good habits you've cultivated in your life.

"*He causes His sun to rise on the evil and the good, and sends rain on the righteous and the unrighteous.*"

Matthew 5:45 NASB

"*Every good thing given and every perfect gift is from above, coming down from the Father of lights, with whom there is no variation or shifting shadow.*"

James 1:17 NASB

✳ **The ABC Formula flows naturally in our lives** and we need to understand how it affects us:

ACTIONS take place.

BELIEFS determine how we view or think about those actions.

CONSEQUENCES that result in your life are primarily based upon your belief, not necessarily on the action that triggered the event.

Dad's Notes

Example:

Someone says something mean to you, such as: "That's a weird outfit you're wearing today."

You believe that they don't like the outfit, *and*

You feel sad and rejected all day.

OR

Someone says, "That's a weird outfit you're wearing today."

You believe that they don't have any taste or style in clothing.

You feel sorry for the person who made the comment, and exhibit confidence in your sense of style.

MORE ABOUT SELF-CONFIDENCE

Feelings of confidence depend upon the type of thoughts you habitually occupy. Think defeat, and you are bound to be defeated.

Norman Vincent Peale

Act as if it were impossible to fail.

Dorothea Brande

Self confidence is the hallmark of a champion...any champion.

Grantland Rice

Your self image need not be permanently damaged by the circumstances of life. It can be recast when there is an infusion of new life in Jesus Christ.

Ed Young

Your core identity—and particularly your perception of it—plays a vital role in determining how you carry yourself in daily life, how much joy you experience, how you treat other people, and how you respond to God.

Josh McDowell

MORE ABOUT GOALS

My policy has always been to ask God to help me set goals because I believe God has a plan for every person.

Bill Bright

The biggest human temptation is to settle for too little.

Thomas Merton

Whatever purpose motivates your life, it must be something big enough and grand enough to make the investment worthwhile.

Warren Wiersbe

Aim at heaven, and you will get earth thrown in. Aim at earth, and you will get neither.

C. S. Lewis

Never run out of goals.

Earl Nightingale

"Without faith a man can do nothing;
with it all things are possible."

———

Sir William Osler

CHAPTER 7

Faith:
Wisdom, Spiritual Truth, and Philosophy

The wisdom, spiritual truth and philosophy of life that you learn and develop as you grow up will, to a large degree, determine the direction your life will take.

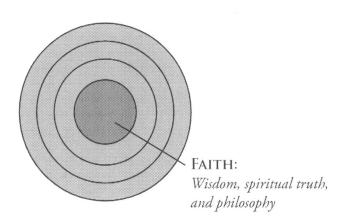

FAITH:
Wisdom, spiritual truth, and philosophy

Dad's Notes

❋ As a Christian I *have:*

- The confidence of salvation and knowledge that my forever is absolutely guaranteed by the promises of Scripture.
- The guidance of the Holy Spirit.
- The eternal wisdom revealed in the Bible.
- An eternal destiny and purpose beyond this life.

❋ Who am I?

According to Scripture:

- I am a new creation in Christ Jesus (II Corinthians 5:17).

- I am fearfully and wonderfully made (Psalm 139:14).

- I can do all things through Christ who strengthens me (Phil 4:13—*Christ confidence* NOT self-confidence).

- I am not only a sinner saved by grace, but a saint being sanctified by the Holy Spirit for the works that Christ has prepared for me (Ephesians 2:8-10).

Dad's Notes

✳ **The benefits of prayer:**

1. Calms me down

2. Helps me organize my thoughts

3. Gives me the chance to ask God for help

4. Helps me gain His perspective on my situation

5. Helps me to walk in the Spirit and become in-tune with God, and helps me more consciously exhibit the fruit of the Spirit

Dad's Notes ✳ **Why pray?**

- To enjoy the spiritual fellowship that results from a more intimate relationship with the Lord.
- It takes our focus off of ourselves and the temporal world we are living in.
- To petition God for the needs of ourselves and others.
- It renews our eternal perspective.
- It builds our faith in Him when we see Him answer those prayers.
- It renews our mind, especially as we focus on praying back to God the promises that he has made to us in scripture. (Hebrews 13:5)
- Sometimes it is to turn the heart of God.
- More often prayer will change our mind and bring us in tune with God's purposes.

❋ Dads who care for their children pray these prayers for their children:

1. You will never take for granted the three spiritual advantages you have:

- Salvation and the promise of heaven.
- The wisdom of the Holy Scripture.
- The presence of the Holy Spirit in your life.

2. That you will select your friends very carefully because *"bad company corrupts good morals"* and *"good company encourages faithfulness"* (1 Corinthians 15:33).

3. That you will say "no" to alcohol, drugs, tobacco and anything that is potentially addictive and will only work to your detriment.

4. That you will be sexually pure until marriage and within those marriage vows.

Dad's Notes

Knowledge is the information, facts and things I have learned.

Wisdom is God's timeless principles and the truth that never changes. It provides us with the ability to apply knowledge. It can also include the experience and lessons learned by others (OPE).

✳ The Law of the Harvest says:
What you sow you shall reap.

✳ God measures a person by putting a "tape measure around their heart."

"But the LORD said to Samuel, 'Do not look at his appearance or at the height of his stature, because I have rejected him; for God sees not as man sees, for man looks at the outward appearance, but the LORD looks at the heart.'"

1 Sam 16:7 NASB

✳ **Even good people will suffer in this life.**

"There was a man in the land of Uz whose name was Job; and that man was blameless, upright, fearing God and turning away from evil."

Job 1:1 NASB

It was because of Job's goodness that he was the target of Satan's attacks as described in the book of Job. Why should we be surprised by suffering in this world?

✳ **Three reasons that we go through trials:**
   To develop our character
   To accomplish His will
   To discipline us

Dad's Notes

❋ **When you die,** and we all will, there are only three things of significance that will be left behind:

- Your family
- You reputation
- Your faith that leads to life eternal

That faith is where you will also find peace, purpose, meaning, and significance.

❋ **Words without life is hypocrisy, but life without words is a mystery.**

"But the fruit of the Spirit is love, joy, peace, patience, kindness, goodness, faithfulness, gentleness, self-control; against such things there is no law. Now those who belong to Christ Jesus have crucified the flesh with its passions and desires."

Galatians 5: 22-23 NASB

✳ What is the fruit of the Spirit?

What are the characteristics that are opposite the fruit of the Spirit?

- Love vs. Hate
- Joy vs. Sadness
- Peace vs. War
- Patience vs. Impatience
- Kindness vs. Selfishness
- Goodness vs. Evil Intent
- Faithfulness vs. Betrayal
- Gentleness vs. Harshness
- Self Control vs. Chaos

How do you get it?

"Christ redeemed us from the curse of the Law, having become a curse for us, for it is written, 'CURSED IS EVERYONE WHO HANGS ON A TREE' in order that in Christ Jesus the blessing of Abraham might come to the Gentiles, so that we would receive the promise of the Spirit through faith."

Galatians 3:13-14 NASB

MORE ABOUT WISDOM

Don't expect wisdom to come into your life like great chunks of rock on a conveyor belt. Wisdom comes privately from God as a byproduct of right decisions, godly reactions, and the application of spiritual principles to daily circumstances.

Charles Swindoll

Knowledge is horizontal. Wisdom is vertical; it comes down from above.

Billy Graham

The process of living seems to consist in coming to realize truths so ancient and simple that, if stated, they sound like barren platitudes. They cannot sound otherwise to those who have not had the relevant experience: that is why there is no real teaching of such truths possible and every generation starts from scratch.

C. S. Lewis

The more wisdom enters our hearts, the more we will be able to trust our hearts in difficult situations.

John Eldredge

More About Prayer

When we pray, we have linked ourselves with Divine purposes, and we therefore have Divine power at our disposal for human living.

E. Stanley Jones

God shapes the world by prayer. The more praying there is in the world, the better the world will be, and the mightier will be the forces against evil.

E. M. Bounds

Pour out your heart to God and tell Him how you feel. Be real, be honest, and when you get it all out, you'll start to feel the gradual covering of God's comforting presence.

Bill Hybels

He who kneels most stands best.

D. L. Moody

On our knees we are the most powerful force on earth.

Billy Graham

"The reality is that fathers have a tremendous influence on the lives of their children—for better or worse."

—

Dr. Ken R. Canfield

CHAPTER 8

Dads
The Good, The Bad, and The Ugly

Dave Boon tells the story of a day that changed his life. It was a beautiful day in Colorado and he was at home working on a technical report for one of his firm's clients. His oldest daughter, four-year-old Denali, walked into his office and watched as he typed away at his computer. He noticed her and said, "Hi. What's up?" With the innocence that only a child has, she asked a question that would turn Dave and his wife June's life right-side-up. It would set into motion a mid-life career change with gut-wrenching impact.

She asked, "Dad? Why don't you play with me anymore?" Dave's a normal guy, so he immediately started reasoning to himself, "I have an important job. My company has an important client with important problems. The company has paid us a lot of money to help them. Don't bother daddy, because I am very busy right now."

But Dave's wisdom overcame the logic going on in his head. He sat in stunned silence, not being able to come up with a reason that would make sense to his four-year-old. So instead of defending his need to work, Dave said, "What would you like to do?"

She answered, "How about helping me catch grasshoppers in the garden?" Dave and June had offered a bounty of one cent per grasshopper that she removed from the vegetable garden.

Dave said, "OK, let's go." He shut down the computer and caught grasshoppers, played Frisbee, played with the dogs, played a variety of games, ate ice cream, and enjoyed the rest of that gorgeous day.

That night after tucking Denali into bed, he went back to his computer and worked through the night. The next morning they went to the Denver Zoo and enjoyed another great day together. He wondered to himself, "Why wasn't I doing this more often? This is what family life is all about, right?"

Sunday night, after putting her to bed again, he went back to finish the report for the client by the Monday morning deadline. The next morning, he intended to deliver the report to the project manager's office but couldn't find him. He asked of his whereabouts and was informed that he had gone on a two-week vacation. Dave realized that he didn't need to have the report done until the manager returned.

"Great," he thought. "Why am I sacrificing time with my family to meet some self-imposed deadline for this project manager's convenience?" The more he thought about it that week, the more he asked the question, "Why?"

It was a good job that provided an increase in income, but it was taking a toll on Dave and his family. He spent the weekend with a friend and mentor, and his wife June, going over his experience. On the following Monday, Dave handed in his two-week's notice.

The *good news* is that there are still fathers, like Dave Boon, who consider being a dad the most significant thing that they will ever do in this lifetime. They are committed and consistent, seek to know their children, provide for and protect their families, love their wives, are great listeners, and endeavor to provide spiritual leadership in their homes. They are men who are fully engaged in being a dad.

The *bad news* is that there aren't enough of us, and the impact on our culture is evident.

The *ugly truth* is that today in the United States there are fewer children being raised in what we have typically considered the nuclear family, consisting of a husband and wife raising the children born to their marital union. We still sense that this is *how it was supposed to be.* In a 1996 survey by Gallup, 90.0 percent of Americans who responded stated that *it is important for children to live in a home with both their mother and father.* Reality is growing further and further from this ideal.

This ideal has been altered by growing rates of divorce, dramatic increases in out-of-wedlock births, more single parent homes, and homes where fathers are absent for a variety of reasons. Of the 73.2 million children under 18 years of age living in the United States in 2004, 67.7 percent (49.6 million) were living with two parents, 27.9 percent (20.4 million) were living with a single parent, and 4.3 percent (3.1 million) were living with neither of their parents.[8] Add to this the challenges and complexities facing fathers, who are dealing with joint parental rights and blended families, and we can quickly get discouraged. Nearly 40 percent of babies born in the United States in 2007 were delivered by unwed mothers, according to data released by the National Center for Health Statistics. The 1.7 million out-of-wedlock births, of 4.3 million total births, marked a more than 25 percent jump from five years prior.

Former President George W. Bush said, *"Over the past four decades, **fatherlessness has emerged as one of our greatest social problems.** We know that children who grow up with absent fathers can suffer lasting damage. They are more likely to end up in poverty or drop out of school, become*

8) *U.S. Census Bureau. Current Population Survey Reports. "Household Relationship and Living Arrangements of Children Under 18 Years, by Age, Sex, Race, Hispanic Origin: 2004, All Races, White only, Black only and Hispanic only." Table C2. Published July 29, 2005 http://www.census.gov/population/socdemo/hh-fam/cps2004/tabC2-all.csv*

addicted to drugs, have a child out of wedlock or end up in prison. Fatherlessness is not the only cause of these things, but our nation must recognize it as an important factor."[9]

In the sixth-grade, Mike Garcia was attending Laurel Elementary School in Fort Collins, Colorado. By this time Dave Boon had become the executive director of Partners of Larimer County, the second largest mentoring program in Colorado for "at-risk" youth. Mike was signed up for the program and Dave was matched up as his "senior partner," the term used for the adult in the mentoring relationship.

Mike's grandmother had urged him to sign up because he didn't have an active father or adult male role model in his life. He was living with his mom, a single mother, at what was considered "poverty level." He was often put in a position of being around drugs and alcohol, and saw his mother physically abused by boyfriends or ex-husbands. Drugs were often sold out of his mother's house, but not his grandmother's. No one in his family had ever gone to college, and despite his being bright and very athletic, Mike was going to be challenged to succeed.

When Mike was 15, between his freshman and sophomore year, his mother was taken hostage by an abusive

9) *Speech at the National Fatherhood Initiatives 4th annual National Summit on Fatherhood in Washington, DC, June 7, 2001.*

ex-husband who was not his father. The SWAT Team was called, and Mike was able to escape the house. However, before the ordeal was over, his mother was shot and killed before the shooter took his own life. Life went from being hard—to unbelievably tough—for Mike overnight. He lost his way, began hanging out with bad people who didn't care about him and who encouraged him to make bad choices.

With his mom gone, Mike was on the street with a group that accepted him, but who made his association with them dependent on peer pressure that was anything but positive. Mike quit school and began breaking into houses, stealing, and carrying a gun. He was living on the street, living hand-to-mouth. The good news is that he was caught, arrested and jailed at the Platte Valley Juvenile Facility. It was good news because it meant that he was no longer on the street, where he was able to victimize and hurt people, and continue down a destructive path.

Mike's grandmother called Dave Boon to let him know that he was in jail. After six court appearances, Mike was sentenced to two years probation and 64 hours of community service. Dave helped Mike get signed up for his service hours and enroll at the Centennial High School, an alternative school program. Not only did Dave and June Boon demonstrate their passion for "at-risk" teens by being mentors, they invited Mike into their home to live with them.

The impact of a dad and mom in Mike's life has obviously helped him to get back on a positive path to reaching his potential. Mike entered Centennial High with a 0.5 GPA, and through the balance of his high school education earned a 3.7 GPA at Centennial. He is only the second person in his family to graduate from high school. He considered learning to weld or joining the Job Corps. Instead, he will be the first person in his family to go to college. In fact, he was accepted to five colleges, offered scholarships to most of them, and also earned two Rotary Scholarships.

Mike attended a Rotary Youth Leadership Award camp for high school students and was chosen as a Junior Counselor for Young RYLA, a leadership camp for 8th graders. At that camp, Mike told his story on stage to 120 campers and 30 staff members. There wasn't a dry eye in the room. He closed his presentation with a song that has a lot of meaning for him: "My Wish," by Rascal Flatts.

"I hope the days come easy and the moments pass slow,
And each road leads you where you want to go,
And if you're faced with a choice and you have to choose,
I hope you choose the one that means the most to you."

Being an engaged dad to your own children is a great place to start. But it will not turn the current epidemic of fatherlessness in our nation. Unless you and I catch the passion that Dave and June Boon have for "at-risk" youth and help the millions of kids who need a positive adult role model, it will simply not change the direction of this generation and our nation. There have always been fatherless kids, but the trend is not improving; and it won't unless men step up to the plate.

In 1838 a man by the name of Moses Carver had moved to Diamond, Missouri to homestead and settle on a 240 acre farm there with his brother Richard. A year later his brother died; and though he was opposed to slavery, he purchased a slave because of the need for help on the farm. The slave was 13 years old and her name was Mary. Over the next ten years, Mary bore four children, including Jim and George. George's father was believed to be a slave from a nearby farm, who later died in an accident before George was even born.

Later, Mary and George were kidnapped and taken to Arkansas. George was returned to the farm, but Mary was never seen again. George was raised by Moses and his wife Susan up until age 11. Then, while attending a school for colored students in Neosho, Missouri, he lived with Andrew and Mariah Watkins.

George later attended Simpson College, and then

earned graduate degrees at Iowa State College, before moving to the all black Tuskegee Institute. He was invited there by Booker T. Washington, the founder, to develop their agricultural school. We know George Washington Carver as the man who used the peanut and sweet potato to revolutionize Southern agriculture in the U.S.

The positive impact that each of us can have on our children, as well as those struggling through life without a dad, can have an impact for generations to come. In your community there is a boy or girl, who needs a surrogate dad to encourage them. Maybe it is through the Boy Scouts, the Boys & Girls Club, a local 4-H program, a local mentoring or school program, or your church. You can make an impact beyond your own immediate family. If you are a dad who is able to take on just one of these "youth with unmet potential" as Dave Boon calls them, please consider taking that step. Our world will be better for it, and you will feel great about your investment in a young life with otherwise unmet potential.

David Blankenhorn, founder and president of the Institute for American Values said, *"If I had to summarize my deepest conviction in this whole area of the family, it would be that every child has a birthright to grow up with a mother and father who love the child and love each other. We see so much childhood pain, and so many social problems, stemming from that basic denial of what children need."*

Can you really make a difference?

A man was walking on the beach and saw that it was littered with thousands of starfish. A little boy was picking up the starfish *one by one* and throwing them into the ocean. He asked the boy, "What are you doing?"

The boy replied, "I'm throwing starfish back into the water. If I leave them here they'll dry up and die."

The man said, "But look how many starfish there are. What you're doing can't possibly make a difference."

As the boy picked up another starfish and threw it into the ocean he said, **"Well, it makes a difference to this one!"**

Coach Tom Osborne, University of Nebraska former football coach and Athletic Director, and his wife Nancy established the Teammates™ Mentoring Program with a mission to positively impact the world by inspiring youth to reach their full potential through mentoring. In Coach Osborne's words; *"Our young people face different challenges today that affect them personally. If we are going to make a difference, we have to get involved with them as one-to-one mentors. We know that through a relationship with one student at a time, we can make a difference, not only in this generation, but for the generations to come."*

We can encourage the fatherless one at a time, and make a difference that will change our lives as well. In the end, maybe that is really what it means to be a dad. I hope that reading *Dad's Class* has encouraged you in some way to invest the time that your son or daughter needs from you. I hope also, that perhaps it has inspired you to encourage a child who really needs a father figure worth emulating, to break the cycle of fatherlessness that his or her family may have experienced for generations.

Join us in this mission by visiting us on the web at www.dadsclass.com. We'll share stories that will encourage and inspire you—as that special person called ***Dad***—in the life of your child, grandchild, foster child, or as a mentor for someone who desperately needs a caring adult to encourage them to learn, grow and become all that God intended them to be.

MIA Dads Equal Disaster

If you'd like to see the statistical importance of dads, just Google "fatherless homes" and prepare yourself for a shock. When you begin the search, you'll be inundated with statistics that are disturbing, disheartening, and downright scary. Kids who come from families-without-dads are at greater risk for just about any problem you can name, including poverty, drug use, behavior disorders, homelessness, emotional problems, pregnancy out-of-wedlock, incarceration, and even suicide. The numbers point out the obvious: Kids need fathers who are present and accounted for. But in today's world, it doesn't always work that way.

According to the Census Bureau, about 35% of births in America are to women who are either separated, widowed, divorced, or never married (2006). And we wonder why we have problems in this country. The answer should be obvious.

But what does this mean to you, a concerned father who is already reading a book about becoming an even better dad? Simply this: When it comes to the fine art of dads-raising-kids, more is better—more time, more contact, more concern, more support, more discipline, more education, and more love. The more you engage your kids, the better.

After all, it's possible to be emotionally absent even if you're living under the same roof with your youngsters. And it's possible—even tempting at times—to become absorbed with work, sports, buddies, TV, or a hundred other things that can siphon off precious time you could otherwise be spending with your family. So don't assume for a moment that the only absent dads are the ones who are physically gone. Emotionally absent fathers are still absent . . . and you should never be counted among their number.

Suggested Reading

Books to train and encourage

Fathering: A Practical Guide for Dads
By Grace Ketterman, M.D.
Beacon Hill Press of Kansas City ©1997

Fathers of Influence
By Matthew Kinne and Snapdragon Group
Honor Books, Cook Communications, Colorado Springs, CO ©2006

How to Win Friends & Influence People
by Dale Carnegie
Pocket Books, a division of Simon & Schuster Inc.
©1936, 1964, 1981

How to Get People to Do Things
by Robert Conklin
Ballantine Books ©1985

It Takes a Dad
by Bill Rodebaugh
Tate Publishing, LLC ©2006

It's Better to Build Boys than to Mend Men
by S. Truett Cathy
Looking Glass Books ©2004

Life's Greatest Lessons—20 Things That Matter Most
by Hal Urban
Fireside Books ©2003

Mentoring: Confidence in Finding a Mentor
and Becoming One
by Bobb Biehl
Broadman & Holman Publishers, Nashville, TN ©1996

My Father My Friend
by David Chadwick
Hendrickson Publishers ©2002

My Wish: Don't Get Swept Away As a Teen
by David Boon
Tantalus Books, Fort Collins, CO ©2008

Outliers: The Story of Success
by Malcolm Gladwell
Little, Brown and Company ©2008

Seven Habits of Highly Effective People
by Stephen Covey
Fireside Books ©1989

She Calls Me Daddy
by Robert Wolgemuth
Tyndale House Publishers, Wheaton, IL ©1996

Take the Risk
by Dr. Ben Carson, M.D.
Zondervan, Grand Rapids Michigan ©2008

The 7 Secrets of Effective Fathers
by Ken R. Canfield, PH.D
Tyndale House Publishers, Wheaton, IL ©1992

The Dad in the Mirror
by Patrick Morley & David Delk
Zondervan, Grand Rapids, MI ©2003

The Jesus Habits
by Jay Dennis
Broadman & Holman Publishers ©2005

The Key to Your Child's Heart
by Gary Smalley
Thomas Nelson Publishers ©1992

The Laws of Lifetime Growth: Always Make Your Future Bigger Than Your Past
by Dan Sullivan
Berrett-Koehler Publishers ©2007

The Purpose Driven Life
by Rick Warren
Zondervan ©2002

What My Parents Did Right
by Gloria Gaither
Howard Publishing, West Monroe, LA ©2002

Words Kids Need to Hear
by David Staal
Zondervan ©2008

Words That Hurt, Words That Heal
by Rabbi Joseph Telushkin
Quill, William Morrow, New York ©1996

Your Story

Take some time and write down your ideas, thoughts, and stories that you feel are important to you and that you want to share with your children.

Acknowledgments

Without the persistent encouragement of my good friend, Steve Bonar, I would never have had the courage or willingness to commit the time required to share the ideas presented here. I'd like to thank my wife, Patty and our children, Sarah, Adam, Dana, Jordan, Sarah II, Chelsea, Bri and Lauren who have encouraged me to pass our Dad's Class experiences and ideas on to others. My new friends, Dave and June Boon, and Mike Garcia have been a special inspiration to encourage me and all dads to look beyond their own immediate family to "save kids' lives" wherever we find them at risk because of parents who are absent.

Special thanks goes to Elaine Penn for her assistance in reviewing this book as it developed, using her gift and command of the English language. She has shown patience in working with me for over twenty years.

Finally, I want to thank friends, Bruce and Maureen Stahr for giving me a place to hide-out to complete the manuscript.

My prayer is that God will bless your efforts as you invest time and wisdom into meaningful conversations with your children, grandchildren and other young people who need the encouragement of a dad.

About the Author

Dennis L. Nun is the father of six and husband to one.

He and his wife Patty were married nine years before being blessed with the first of their six children. Desiring to be a fully-engaged father, he set out to spend intentional one-on-one time with each of his children. His approach to Dad's Class can provide you with a template to use in being the father that your children and your spouse need for you to be.